My
Pinterest™

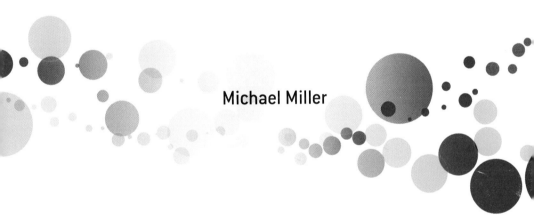

Michael Miller

que®

800 East 96th Street,
Indianapolis, Indiana 46240 USA

My Pinterest

ISBN-13: 978-0-7897-4981-9
ISBN-10: 0-7897-4981-5

Library of Congress Cataloging-in-Publication Data is on file.

Printed in the United States of America

First Printing: May 2012

Trademarks

Warning and Disclaimer

Bulk Sales

Que Publishing offers excellent discounts on this book when ordered in quantity for bulk purchases or special sales. For more information, please contact

U.S. Corporate and Government Sales
1-800-382-3419
corpsales@pearsontechgroup.com

For sales outside of the U.S., please contact

International Sales
international@pearsoned.com

EDITOR-IN-CHIEF
Greg Wiegand

ACQUISITIONS EDITOR
Laura Norman

DEVELOPMENT EDITOR
Charlotte Kughen

MANAGING EDITOR
Kristy Hart

PROJECT EDITOR
Anne Goebel

SENIOR INDEXER
Cheryl Lenser

PROOFREADER
Kathy Ruiz

PUBLISHING
COORDINATOR
Cindy Teeters

COVER DESIGNER
Anne Jones

COMPOSITOR
TnT Design, Inc.

Contents at a Glance

Appendix A, "Understanding Pinterest's Terms of Use," can be found online at quepublishing.com/register.

AUG   2012

Table of Contents

About the Author

Michael Miller is a prolific and popular writer of nonfiction books, known for his ability to explain complex topics to everyday readers. He writes about a variety of topics, including technology, business, and music. His best-selling books include *Facebook for Grown-Ups*, *Absolute Beginner's Guide to Computer Basics*, *The Complete Idiot's Guide to Google+*, *Sams Teach Yourself TweetDeck in 10 Minutes*, and *The Ultimate Digital Music Guide*. Worldwide, his books have sold more than 1 million copies.

Find out more at the author's website: **www.molehillgroup.com**

Follow the author on Pinterest: **www.pinterest.com/molehillgroup/**

Follow the author on Twitter: **molehillgroup**

Dedication

To all the women in my life, most especially my lovely wife Sherry, stepdaughters Kristi, Laura, and Amy, and granddaughters Alethia and Hayley. Oh, and to my mom and sister, too.

Acknowledgments

Thanks to all the folks at Que who helped turn this manuscript quite quickly into a book, including Laura Norman, Charlotte Kughen, and Greg Wiegand.

We Want to Hear from You!

As the reader of this book, *you* are our most important critic and commentator. We value your opinion and want to know what we're doing right, what we could do better, what areas you'd like to see us publish in, and any other words of wisdom you're willing to pass our way.

As an editor-in-chief for Que Publishing, I welcome your comments. You can email or write me directly to let me know what you did or didn't like about this book[md]as well as what we can do to make our books better.

Please note that I cannot help you with technical problems related to the topic of this book. We do have a User Services group, however, where I will forward specific technical questions related to the book.

When you write, please be sure to include this book's title and author as well as your name, email address, and phone number. I will carefully review your comments and share them with the author and editors who worked on the book.

Email: feedback@quepublishing.com

Mail: Greg Wiegand
            Editor-in-Chief
            Que Publishing
            800 East 96th Street
            Indianapolis, IN 46240 USA

Reader Services

Visit our website and register this book at quepublishing.com/register for convenient access to any updates, downloads, or errata that might be available for this book.

Pinboard

Other images from
same web page

Pinned image

In this prologue, you learn about Pinterest—
the latest social network on the Web.

→ Learn what Pinterest is and what it does
→ Discover how Pinterest got started
→ Find out who's using Pinterest and what they're pinning
→ Determine whether or not you should be using Pinterest

Getting to Know Pinterest: What It Is and What It Does

Pinterest is the newest social network around, a collection of virtual online "pinboards" that people use to share pictures they find interesting. Users "pin" photos and other images to their personal message boards and then share their pins with online friends. And when you pin interesting items, you get the site's name—pin+interest = Pinterest.

Sounds interesting, and it must be, because users are spending more time on Pinterest than they are on Google+, LinkedIn, and Twitter—combined. Pinterest is big and getting bigger every month, there's no doubt about it.

What Is Pinterest?

Pinterest is a visually oriented social network. A social network is a website community designed for sharing and communication between users; the top social networks today include Facebook, Google+, and LinkedIn.

In a way, Pinterest is kind of like Facebook but with only pictures. Members can use Pinterest to share photos and other images they find interesting with their family and online friends.

Here's how it works. You start by finding an image on a web page that you like and want to share. You click a "Pin It" button that Pinterest adds to your browser's bookmarks bar, or click the Add button on the Pinterest site, and the selected image is "pinned" to one of your personal online pinboards (which are like old fashioned corkboards, except online).

A pinboard becomes a place where you can create and share collections of those things you like or find interesting. You can have as many pinboards as you like, organized by category or topic. Pinterest creates a few default pinboards for you when you first sign up (such as Products I Love and My Style), but you can also create your own custom pinboards, built around your favorite topics and interests.

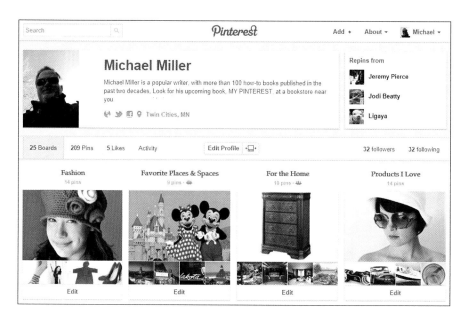

Friends who follow you see the images you pin, and you see the ones they pin. You can also "like" other people's pins, and repin their items to your pinboards, thus repeating the original pin. It's a very visual way to share things you like, online.

Sharing on Other Social Networks

Sharing on Pinterest isn't limited to other Pinterest uses. You can also configure Pinterest to automatically post your pins to your Facebook and Twitter accounts. Learn more in Chapter 11, "Sharing Pins to Facebook and Twitter."

Like most social networks today, Pinterest is free to use. You can access Pinterest from any web browser, or from your mobile phone.

Pinterest Mobile

There is a Pinterest app for the iPhone, so you can pin on the go. Learn more in Chapter 13, "Using Pinterest on Your iPhone."

How Pinterest Got Started

Pinterest might seem like a brand new site, but it was actually launched (for closed beta testing) in March 2010. It was developed by a small Silicon Valley company called Cold Brew Labs, founded by Ben Silbermann, Evan Sharp, and Paul Sciarra. Silbermann was a former product specialist at Google, Sharp a product designer at Facebook, and Sciarra came from the world of venture capital. That combination of talents was uniquely suited to creating a new visual social network.

Cold Brew launched in 2008 as a mobile shopping startup, but nothing really came of that. With the success of Facebook and social networking, the company changed its focus to what it then dubbed "social cataloging," and Pinterest was born.

Still in beta testing, Pinterest was named one of the "50 Best Websites of 2011" by *TIME Magazine* in August 2011. That exposure helped to fuel an explosion of interest in the Pinterest website, and a corresponding increase in traffic followed. In June 2011, Pinterest had just a half million users; by January 2012, comScore reported that the user base had grown to more than 11.7 million users. Pinterest had become the fastest site in history to break through the 10 million user mark—despite remaining in a public testing phase with membership via invitation only.

Who's Using Pinterest?

If you're wondering who is using Pinterest, at this point in time it's primarily a woman's world. Pinterest users are overwhelmingly female (80%), mainly between the ages of 25 and 44 (55%), and have incomes between $25,000 and $75,000 (69%). This explains Pinterest's popularity among "mommy bloggers" and the arts community.

These demographics also make Pinterest attractive to businesses, which are increasingly using Pinterest to market their brands and products online. Already, Pinterest is driving more traffic to company websites and blogs than YouTube, Google+, and LinkedIn combined. Shareaholic's January 2012 Referral Traffic Report ranks Pinterest as statistically equal with Twitter and Google in driving referrals, behind only Facebook and StumbleUpon.

More importantly, Pinterest users are highly engaged with the site; they really like it and use it a lot. Pinterest users spend an average of 98 minutes per month on the site, which compares to 5 minutes per month for Google+ users, 16 minutes/month for LinkedIn users, and 24 minutes/month for Twitter users. The only social media with more engagement are Facebook and Tumblr.

What Do People Pin?

Pinterest fosters visual sharing of both images and videos. The average user pins product photos, of course, as well as recipes, slogans, and other items that can be presented visually.

Some users think of Pinterest as an idea factory. These people post pictures of things they'd like to purchase, or of designs they'd like to implement in their home. That means lots of photos of dream bathrooms, designer clothing, fashion accessories, and the like.

You also find a lot of photos of fashions and food, the latter accompanied by step-by-step recipes. Also popular are photos of crafts and other do-it-yourself projects, as well as collectible items.

In addition, Pinterest is becoming a big hangout for both professional and amateur photographers. Where better to share the photos you take than on the pinboards of a visual social network?

For that matter, many people use Pinterest to share family photos, much like a photoblog or online scrapbook. It's as easy to upload a photo to pin as it is to pin something you find on the Web.

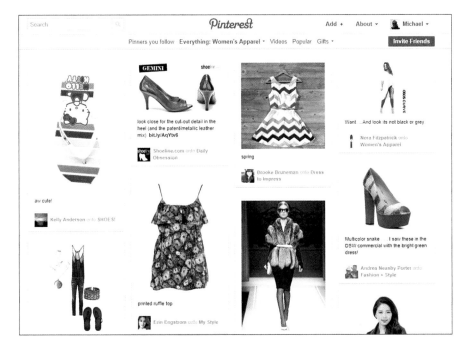

The bottom line is that you can pin anything you find interesting to a Pinterest pinboard. If you're into classic movies, pin cast photos or movie posters to your pinboard. If you collect vintage coins, pin photos of those coins. If you're a fashion buff, pin pictures of this season's hottest designer clothes. If you're into cars, pin beauty shots of your favorite models. If you fancy yourself a gourmet cook, pin pictures of your favorite dishes. If you're looking to spread cheer, pin funny or inspiring photos. The sky's the limit.

Should You Be Interested in Pinterest?

Is Pinterest a site you should be using? Millions of people have decided it's a site for them.

If you like to share items you find funny or that interest or inspire you, Pinterest is the place to do it. A lot of people already use Facebook in this fashion, posting images instead of text posts. It's easier to post images to Pinterest, though, because the site itself was designed with visual sharing in mind. You can find an eyeful of interesting items when you browse your friends' pinboards, and they, in turn, can get a lot of inspiration from what you pin.

It helps that Pinterest is so easy to use. It focuses on one thing only (images), which makes it more focused than Facebook or Google+. Pinning a new item takes a simple click of the mouse, and browsing your friends' latest pins is something you can do over your morning coffee.

So for purely visual sharing of things you find interesting, Pinterest is the way to go. Set up a (free) account, start following a few friends, and see how easy it is to find fun and useful stuff. You can then start pinning a few things yourself, and keep going as fast and as far as you like.

IS PINTEREST A FACEBOOK KILLER?

Facebook is the big dog in the world of social networking, with 800 million users. At 11 million users, Pinterest is barely a blip on Facebook's radar, but it's growing fast and getting a lot of positive attention.

Given Pinterest's rapid growth and glowing reviews, is it possible that Pinterest will eventually replace Facebook? Probably not, but it certainly could supplement the larger site. After all, Pinterest doesn't do all the things that Facebook does; you can't share long text messages on Pinterest (it's for images only), nor can you play games and run apps as you can on Facebook. So you still need Facebook for that sort of thing.

But Pinterest is much more efficient and effective for visual sharing than Facebook is. It's possible that Facebook users will start using Pinterest to share their photos and other visual items, and leave Facebook for more text-based sharing and communication. And remember, anything you pin on Pinterest can be shared on Facebook (and Twitter), too. The two social networks are made to co-exist.

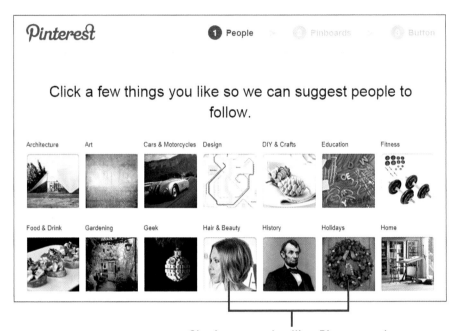

Signing up and selling Pinterest what you're interested in

In this chapter, you learn how to request an invitation to join Pinterest (it's invitation-only at this stage), use your Facebook or Twitter credentials to create a new Pinterest account, and set up your account by following some people and creating pinboards that you'll post to.

→ Requesting an invitation
→ Signing up for a new account
→ Setting up your account

1

Signing Up for a Pinterest Account

Pinterest is the hot new social network that lets you share images and videos you find interesting. You need to join Pinterest to use the site, but membership is free.

Soliciting an Invitation

As of March 2012, Pinterest is still technically in a public testing phase. That means that the site is not open to the general public; membership is by invitation only. You can request an invitation from the Pinterest site, or you can ask a current Pinterest user to send you an invitation.

Unlimited Invitations
A Pinterest user can send out an unlimited number of invitations for new members.

>>>step-by-step

Requesting an Invitation

You can request an invitation directly from Pinterest by following these steps:

1. Use your web browser to go to the Pinterest website, located at www.pinterest.com.

2. Click the red Request an Invite button.

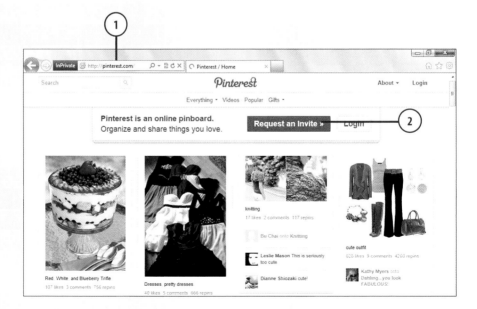

3. Enter your email address into the text box.

4. Click the blue Request Invitation button.

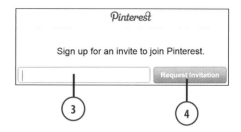

It's Not All Good

Some users have experienced a relatively fast response from requesting an invitation, with responses in less than a week. Other users have received no response from this type of request and have had to resort to soliciting invitations from current Pinterest users.

>>>step-by-step

Sending an Invitation

Within Pinterest, a current user can send you an invitation by using the following steps. After you have your own Pinterest account, you can use these steps to send invitations to others:

1. Mouse over your name in the top-right corner of any Pinterest page.

2. Select Invite Friends from the drop-down menu.

3. Enter the email address of the friend you want to invite into the Email Address 1 box on the Invite Your Friends to Pinterest page.

4. Enter additional email addresses for other friends into the other Email Address boxes.

5. Enter an optional personal note to your friends into the Add a Personal Note box.

6. Click the Send Invites button.

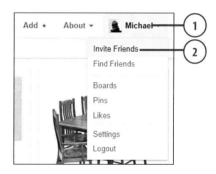

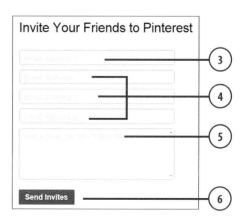

Creating a Pinterest Account

After you receive an invitation, you can sign up for your own personal Pinterest account. There is no charge to create an account; using Pinterest is completely free. You do, however, have to have a Facebook or Twitter account to sign up for Pinterest.

Facebook or Twitter Account Needed

You use your existing Facebook or Twitter account to sign up for Pinterest. If you do not yet have a Facebook or Twitter account, you need to establish one first. (They're free, too.)

>>>step-by-step

Signing Up with a Facebook Account

You receive your Pinterest invitation via email. Follow these steps to sign up using your existing Facebook account:

1. Click the sign up link in the email invitation.

2. Click the Sign Up with Facebook button on the congratulations page that opens in your web browser.

3. On the Facebook Login page, enter the email address and password you use to sign into Facebook and then click the Log In button.

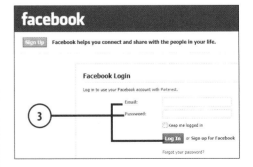

4. Click the green Go to App button on the Pinterest app page.

5. Create a new account on the Pinterest site. Enter your desired username into the Username box.

6. Enter your email address into the Email box.

7. Enter your desired password into the Password box.

8. Click the blue Create Account button.

You are now prompted to set up your Pinterest account. Skip to the "Telling Pinterest More About Yourself" section to continue.

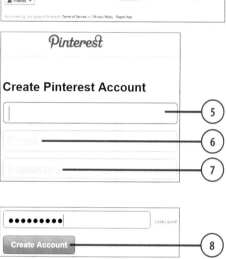

It's Not All Good

KEEPING PRIVATE INFO PRIVATE

When you sign up for Pinterest with your Facebook account, you're giving Pinterest permission to retrieve information about yourself from your Facebook account, and to post to your Facebook timeline and news feed. If you'd rather keep some of this personal information private, you need to reconfigure the privacy settings in both Pinterest and Facebook. Learn more in Chapter 11, "Sharing Pins to Facebook and Twitter."

>>>step-by-step

Signing Up with a Twitter Account

You can also sign into Pinterest with a Twitter account.

1. Click the sign up link in the email invitation.

2. Click the Sign Up with Twitter link on the congratulations page that opens in your web browser.

3. Enter the username or email address and password you use to sign into Twitter on the Authorize Pinterest to Use Your Account? page and then click the Sign In button.

4. Create a new Pinterest account. Enter your desired username into the Username box.

5. Enter your email address into the Email box.

6. Enter your desired password into the Password box.

7. Click the blue Create Account button.

Telling Pinterest More About Yourself

After you've created a new Pinterest account, you're prompted to enter some basic information about yourself in order to set up your account. That's because Pinterest needs to know a little about the kinds of things you like in order to suggest people you might want to follow and provide ways for you to organize your own pins.

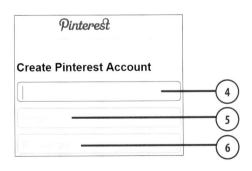

>>>step-by-step

1. On the Pinterest People page, click one or more topics in which you're interested.

2. Click the blue Follow People button at the bottom of the page to proceed.

3. Pinterest signs you up to follow ten people who share the interests you selected. To not follow any of these people, click the Unfollow button next to their names.

4. Click the blue Create Boards button to proceed.

5. Pinterest suggests five topics for your initial pinboards: Products I Love, Favorite Places & Spaces, Books Worth Reading, My Style, and For the Home. Edit the name of any of these boards by positioning your cursor at the end of the name and using the Backspace key to erase the name one letter at a time. Use your keyboard to retype a new or edited name.

6. Delete any of the suggested pinboards by mousing over the pinboard name and clicking the X.

7. Click the Add button to add a different pinboard. This displays a new, blank text box; enter the name of the new pinboard into this box.

8. Click the blue Create button to proceed.

9. Pinterest creates the pinboards and displays a page that talks about creating a Pin It button. Turn to Chapter 6, "Pinning to Pinterest," to learn more about creating this button. Click the blue Start Pinning! at the bottom of the page to begin using Pinterest.

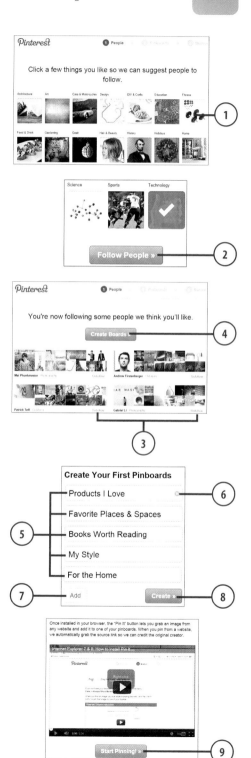

Search
box

Click to go to
home page

Navigation
bar

Filter
bar

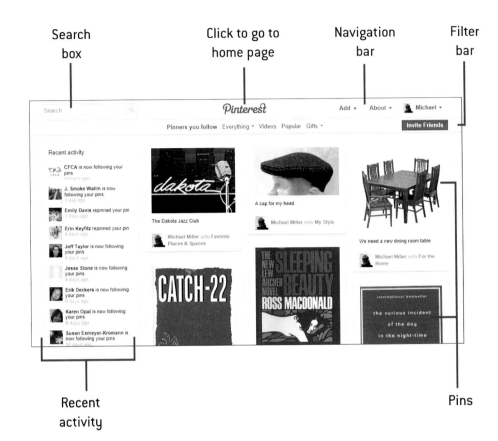

Recent
activity

Pins

In this chapter, you learn how to find your way around the Pinterest site—and how to get help if you need it.

→ Logging into and out of your Pinterest account
→ Finding your way around the Pinterest site
→ Getting help
→ Reading the official Pinterest blog

Navigating Pinterest

Pinterest is a relatively easy website to get around. After you've logged on, it's a simple matter of displaying certain types of pins from certain users and then knowing how to get back to the main page.

Pinterest's home page displays lots of interesting pins, of course, but it also includes a "ticker" of your recent activity in the left sidebar. It's a good way to keep track of new friends that you're following—or who are following you.

Logging Into and Out of Pinterest

After you've created your Pinterest account, you can log into Pinterest at any time.

>>>step-by-step

Logging Into Pinterest

You can log into Pinterest with the email address and password you created when you signed up, or with your Facebook or Twitter credentials. Follow these steps:

1. Use your web browser to go to the Pinterest website, located at www.pinterest.com.

2. Click the Login button or link.

3. To log in with your Pinterest credentials, enter your email address into the Email Address box, your password into the Password box, and then click the Login button.

4. If you are currently logged into Facebook, you can log in with your Facebook credentials by clicking the Login with Facebook button.

5. If you are currently logged into Twitter, you can log in with your Twitter credentials by clicking the Login with Twitter button.

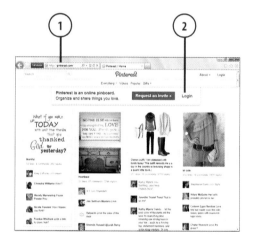

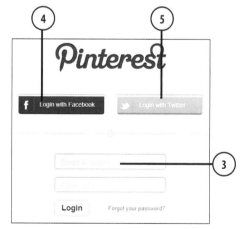

Logging Out of Pinterest

When you're done using Pinterest for the day, you can log out of your Pinterest account by following these steps:

1. Click your name at the top-right corner of any Pinterest page.

2. Select Logout from the drop-down menu.

Stay Logged In

There's really no good reason to manually log out of Pinterest. Many users stay logged in whenever they're using their computers; this makes it easier to pin new images to your pinboards.

Getting to Know the Pinterest Interface

Pinterest has an easy-to-grasp interface. The home page consists of a two-tier menu bar at the top, with individual pins filling up the bulk of the page beneath that.

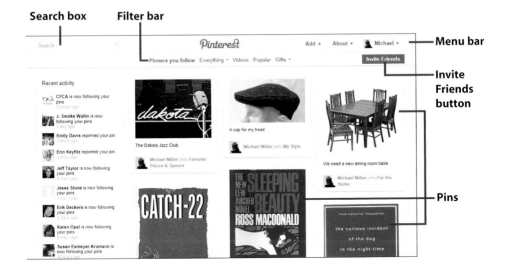

Understanding the Menu Bar

You use the menu bar to navigate around the Pinterest site. There are actually two tiers of menus; one sits on top of the other.

The top tier of the menu bar is visible on every page of the Pinterest site. It consists of the following elements that help you navigate the site and manage your account:

- Search box (searches the site)

- Pinterest logo (click to return to home page)

- Add+ menu (adds new pins and pinboards)

- About menu (displays information about Pinterest)

- *Yourname* menu (view and manage details of your account)

The bottom tier of the menu bar is present only when you're viewing Pinterest's home page. This bar consists of the following elements that help you filter the types of pins displayed. Click any item to display corresponding pins:

- Pinners you follow

- Everything (mouse over to filter pins by category)

- Videos

- Popular

- Gifts (mouse over to filter pins by price range)

>>>step-by-step

Using the Menu Bar

You use the top tier of the menu bar to navigate and perform various functions on the Pinterest site.

1. Click the Add+ button to add a new pin to a pinboard, upload a pin from your computer, or create a new pinboard.

2. Mouse over the About menu and make a selection from the drop-down list to access Pinterest's help system, read the Pinterest blog, or view additional informa- tion about Pinterest.

3. Mouse over your name at the far right of the menu bar and make a selection from the drop-down list to invite new friends to use Pinterest; find friends from exist- ing members; view your own pins, boards, and likes; configure your account settings; or log out from the Pinterest site.

4. Click the Pinterest logo to return to the Pinterest home page.

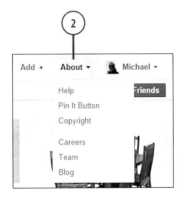

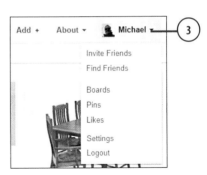

Getting Help

Pinterest includes a rudimentary help system with information about typical operation and common problems. Pinterest also has a company blog that presents the latest company news and information.

>>>step-by-step

Viewing Pinterest's Help System

Pinterest's help system consists of answers to a series of questions about the site.

1. Mouse over the About item in the menu bar.

2. Click Help from the drop-down menu.

3. The Help page displays a number of common questions about using Pinterest. To view an answer for a given question, click that question.

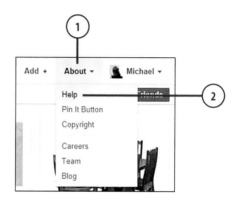

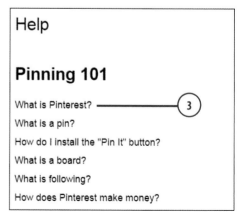

Reading the Pinterest Blog

Recent news about Pinterest and advice on how to use the site are posted to the official Pinterest blog.

1. Mouse over the About item in the menu bar.

2. Click Blog from the drop-down menu.

3. The most recent blog posts are displayed at the top of the page. Click a category in the left column to view posts about specific topics.

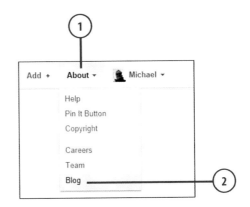

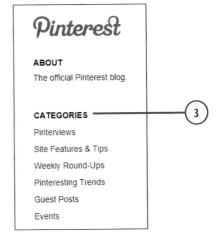

Filter bar   Click here to display   Categories
                         home page

In this chapter, you learn how to find inter-esting items on Pinterest by browsing and searching.

→ Browsing Pinterest's home page
→ Browsing Pinterest by category
→ Searching Pinterest for pins, pinboards, and people
→ Viewing and clicking pins

Browsing and Searching for Pinteresting Items

How do you find items of interest on Pinterest? There are two ways to do it, by browsing or by searching. You can find many items worth viewing with both approaches.

Of course, you can also find interesting items by browsing your friends' pinboards. Chances are you have similar tastes; it's all about the social sharing.

Browsing Pinterest

The first place to look for interesting items is Pinterest's home page. You can view this page at any time by clicking the Pinterest logo at the top of any page.

>>>step-by-step

Browsing Pinterest's Home Page

Pinterest's home page can display a variety of items, depending on what you select at the top of the page—Pinners You Follow, Everything, Videos, Popular, and Gifts. All pins are in reverse chronological order—the most recent items appear at the top of the page.

When you reach the bottom of the page, Pinterest automatically loads more pins, so you can scroll continuously. Just keep scrolling to view more items.

How Many Columns Wide?

The Pinterest home page (all pages that display pins, actually) is organized in a series of columns. How many columns you see depends on the width of your web browser. Four columns is the minimum, and in fact you can cut off the fourth column if your browser window isn't wide enough. Make the browser wider and you'll see a fifth column, then a sixth.

Here's how you determine what is displayed on the home page:

1. Click the Pinterest logo at the top of any page to go to the home page.

2. By default, the home page displays pins from people you follow. If Pinterest is not displaying these pins, click Pinners You Follow at the top of the page.

Recent Activity

The top of the far-left column on the Pinners You Follow page is devoted to your recent activity—new people you're following, new people who are following you, and so forth. Additional pins are displayed beneath the Recent Activity box.

3. To display pins from all users, click Everything.

4. To display only those pins of video items, click Videos.

5. To display the most popular pins on the site, click Popular.

6. To display pins of potential gift items, click Gifts. (The price of each gift item is bannered in the top-left corner of the image.)

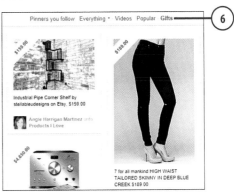

Browsing Pinterest by Category

You can also browse pins within a given topic category. For example, you can browse all pins related to Architecture, Art, or Women's Apparel.

To view pins by category, follow these steps:

1. Click the Pinterest logo at the top of any page to go to the home page.

2. Mouse over the Everything item on the menu bar to display the drop-down list of categories.

3. Click the category you want to browse. Pinterest displays the most recent pins for that category.

Searching Pinterest

Given the large number of pins in all categories, browsing may not be the most effective way to find pins you're interested in. Instead, you can search the Pinterest site for pins about a specific topic; you can also search for topic-oriented pinboards or for pins from a specific person.

Conducting a Search by Topic

Searching Pinterest is as easy as entering a query and pressing the Enter key on your keyboard.

1. Enter one or more keywords that describe what you're looking for into the search box at the top of any Pinterest page.

2. Press the Enter key or click the magnifying glass button next to the search box.

Keywords and Queries

A *keyword* is simply a word that describes something you're looking for. All the keywords you enter comprise your *query*. For example, if you're looking for items related to rock gardening, you would enter the keywords **rock** and **gardening**. Taken together, **rock gardening** is your query.

3. Pinterest returns the first page of search results—those pins that match your query. Scroll down the page to view additional items.

4. Click Boards at the top of the results page to display pinboards about this topic instead of displaying individual pins.

5. Click the Follow button to follow new pins to a selected pinboard.

6. Click a board's graphic to view the contents of that pinboard.

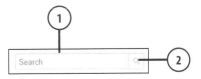

>>>*step-by-step*

Conducting a Search for a Pinterest User

You can also search Pinterest for pins from a specific user.

1. Enter the person's first and last name or username (if you know it) into the search box at the top of any Pinterest page.

2. Press the Enter key or click the magnifying glass button next to the search box. Pinterest returns the first page of search results; this page typically displays individual pins from people who match your query.

3. Click People at the top of the results page to display only individual users, not pins. Pinterest displays those users who match your query.

4. Click the Follow button for a user to follow that person on Pinterest.

5. Click a person's name or picture to view that person's Pinterest page.

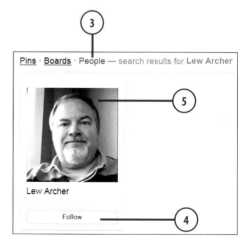

Personal Pages

A Pinterest user's personal page includes all the pinboards that person has created, as well as information about that user.

Viewing a Pin

A pin is an image or video that a user "pins" to her virtual pinboard on the Pinterest site. In addition to showing photographs or other images, a pin also links to a page that displays more information about the pin—including a link to the web page on which the image originally appeared.

A typical pin includes the following elements:

- The image that is pinned

- A short text description from the person who pinned the image

- The name of the person who pinned the image

- The name of the person's pinboard to which the image was pinned

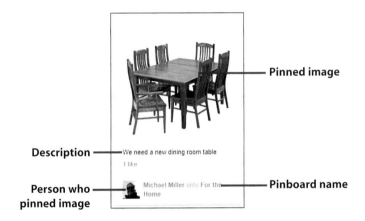

If others have commented on a pin, their comments appear beneath the pinned image. If comments are present, a Comment box is also displayed; you can comment on the pin by entering your message into the Add a Comment box and then pressing Return.

>>>*step-by-step*

Clicking a Pin

You can click the various elements of a pin to go to other parts of the Pinterest site. Follow these steps:

1. Click the person's name beneath the pinned image to view the pinner's personal Pinterest page.

2. Click the pinboard's name beneath the pinned image to view the pinner's pinboard to which the image is pinned.

3. Repin, like, or comment on a pin by mousing over the pinned image to display these additional buttons and then click the button for the desired action.

Repins, Likes, and Comments

Learn more about repins, likes, and comments, see Chapter 9, "Liking, Repinning, and Commenting."

---

4. To view more information about the item, click the pinned image. The pin page displays a variety of information and links for additional activities.

5. Click the pinned image to view the original web page for this item.

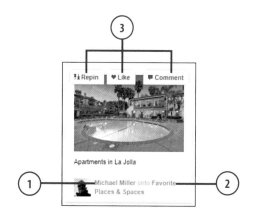

6. Enter your thoughts into the Add a Comment box to comment on the pinned item. Click the Post Comment button when done.

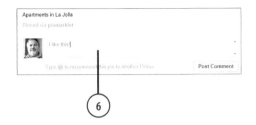

7. Scroll to the board panel in the top-left corner (in Internet Explorer) or the Pinned Onto the Board panel (in Google Chrome) to view other items that have been pinned to this pinboard.

8. Scroll to the Also from *website* (in Internet Explorer) or Pinned from *website* (in Google Chrome) section to view other items that have been pinned from the same original website.

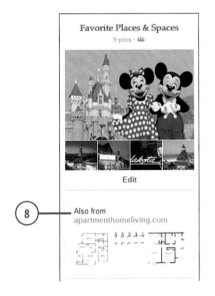

Reporting a Pin

Occasionally you'll find pins that are somehow offensive (typically adult content) or that are blatant spam. When you find a pin that you feel shouldn't be on a pinboard, you can report the pin to Pinterest for further action.

1. Click the pin's image to go to the pin's information page.

2. Click the Report Pin button on the right side of the page.

3. Select the reason for reporting this pin—Nudity or Pornography, Attacks a Group or Individual, Graphic Violence, Hateful Speech or Symbols, Spam, or Other.

4. Click the red Report Pin button.

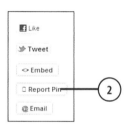

Great room.

Michael Miller onto Favorite Places & Spaces

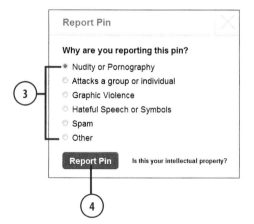

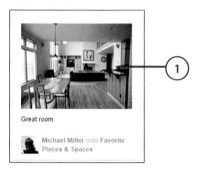

REPORTING COPYRIGHT VIOLATIONS

You can also report a pin if it's an image to which you own the copyright. To do this, click the pin to go to the pin's information page and then click the Report Pin button. When the Report Pin dialog box appears, click the Is This Your Intellectual Property? link. This displays a page with more information about reporting copyright violations, and a button that links to Pinterest's Copyright Complaint Form. Follow the instructions on this page to report the copyright violation.

Personal profile

Click to follow this person

In this chapter, you learn how to follow all
the pins your friends make on Pinterest.

→ Understanding how following works
→ Finding and following friends
→ Following individual pinboards
→ Unfollowing friends and pinboards

Following (and Unfollowing) Others on Pinterest

You can use Pinterest to find items of interest from any user.
You can also use Pinterest to keep abreast of the items that
your friends like by following the pins your friends make. You
can follow all the pins from a given person, or only those pins
made to a specific pinboard.

Understanding Following

When you find someone who posts a lot things you're interested in, you can *follow* that person on Pinterest. Following a person means that all that person's new pins display on your Pinterest home page.

Pins on Your Home Page

You display the Pinterest home page by clicking the Pinterest logo at the top of any page. You can then display pins from the people you follow by clicking Pinners You Follow at the top of the home page.

Pinterest follows all the pinboards a person creates, not just the boards that exist when you first choose to follow that person. When that person creates a new pinboard, you automatically follow the pins to that board, too.

When you follow people on Pinterest, they're notified that you're following them, and they can choose to follow you in return. You can, at any time, opt to *unfollow* a person—that is, to not see that person's posts any more. When you unfollow a person, she is *not* notified of this.

In addition to following individual people, you can also follow individual pinboards. This way you can see new pins about a given topic without having to also see unrelated pins from a person who posts to that pinboard.

Finding and Following Friends

Before you can start following other users on Pinterest, you first have to find people you want to follow. There are a number of ways to do this:

- You can browse your Facebook friends list for those who are using Pinterest and choose to follow any of them.

- You can search Pinterest for people by name and then choose to follow them.

- You can search Pinterest for pins about a given topic and then choose to follow those users who pinned items you liked.

- You can invite people not currently using Pinterest to sign up for Pinterest and then follow them.

>>>step-by-step

Finding Facebook Friends to Follow

Pinterest is closely connected to the Facebook social network. If you've opted to link your Pinterest and Facebook accounts, it's easy to find Facebook friends who are also using Pinterest.

1. Mouse over your name in the top right corner of any Pinterest page.

2. Select Find Friends from the drop-down menu.

3. If you haven't yet connected your Pinterest and Facebook accounts, you need to click the Find Friends from Facebook button and, when prompted, log into your Facebook account.

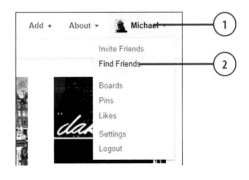

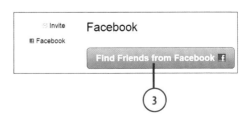

4. Pinterest displays all your Facebook friends. Those who are already using Pinterest are displayed in the right Friends on Pinterest column and have Follow buttons next to their names. Click the Follow button to follow a person.

5. Facebook friends who are not yet members of Pinterest are displayed in the left Invite Friends column and have Invite buttons next to their names. Click the Invite button to invite a person to join Pinterest.

6. Click the Send Request button when the Send This Pinterest Request dialog box appears. Your friend will receive a Pinterest invitation via Facebook.

Searching for Friends to Follow

If you have a friend who is already using Pinterest, you can search the Pinterest user base for that person and then choose to follow her.

1. Enter the person's first and last name or username (if you know it) into the search box at the top of any Pinterest page.

2. Press the Enter key or click the magnifying glass button next to the search box.

3. Click People at the top of the search results page. The person you searched for should be listed on this page.

4. Click the Follow button to follow that user.

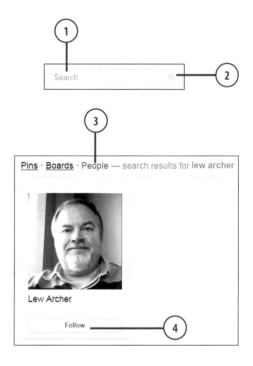

>>>step-by-step

Searching for People Who Make Interesting Posts

You often find people to follow by first noting one or more interesting pins they've made. If you find a pin that grabs your attention, you can follow the person who pinned that item.

1. Navigate to the pin that interests you.

2. Click the person's name beneath the pin to display his or her personal Pinterest page.

3. Click the Follow All button beneath the person's profile.

Classy

Michael Miller onto My Style

Friends of Friends

Another way to find people to follow is to look at who your friends follow, or who follows your friends. When you click a person's name to go to their personal Pinterest page, click either the Followers or Following links under the person's name in the left sidebar. You'll then see a list of people who follow this person or whom this friend is following, respectively. You can follow any of these once-removed "friends" by clicking the Follow button next to his or her name.

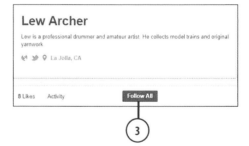

Lew Archer

Lew is a professional drummer and amateur artist. He collects model trains and original yarnwork

La Jolla, CA

8 Likes   Activity   Follow All

Inviting Friends to Follow via Email

If you have a real-world friend whom you think might make interesting pins but who does not yet belong to Pinterest, you can invite her to join the Pinterest community—and then follow her pins. Follow these steps to invite a new member:

1. Mouse over your name in the top-right corner of any Pinterest page.

2. Select Invite Friends from the drop-down menu. The Invite Your Friends to Pinterest page displays.

3. Enter the email address of the friend you want to invite into the Email Address 1 box.

4. Enter an optional personal note to your friend into the Add a Personal Note box.

5. Click the Send Invites button.

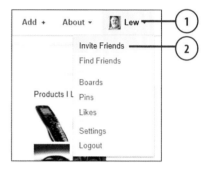

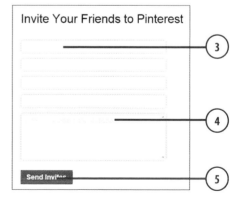

How to Follow—or Unfollow—a Friend

Opting to follow a person's pins on Pinterest is as easy as clicking a button.

>>>step-by-step

Following a Friend

After you've located a person, you can follow that person by following these steps:

1. Go to the user's personal Pinterest page.

2. Click the Follow All button.

Lew Archer

Lew is a professional drummer and amateur artist. He collects model trains and original yarnwork

La Jolla, CA

8 Likes   Activity   Follow All

Following the Contents of a Pinboard

Instead of following all of a person's pins, you can instead follow only a specific pinboard. When you do this, you see new pins made by this person to the selected pinboard, but you don't see pins made to other pinboards.

1. Go to the user's personal Pinterest page.

2. Click the Follow button for the pinboard you want to follow.

>>>step-by-step

Unfollowing a Friend

Over time, you may determine that you're really not all that interested in a given friend's pins. In this instance, you can choose to unfollow this person, so that you don't see any new pins posted. Follow these steps:

1. Click your name at the top-right corner of any Pinterest page. Your personal page displays.

2. Click Following under your name to see a list of all the people you're following on Pinterest.

3. Click the Unfollow button next to the person you no longer want to follow.

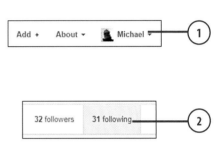

Unfollowing a Pinboard

You might also find that you're no longer interested in the pins made to a given pinboard. You can, at any time, opt to unfollow pins to this board.

1. Click your name at the top-right corner of any Pinterest page. Your personal page displays.

2. Click Following under your name in the left sidebar to see a list of all the people you're following on Pinterest.

3. Click the name of the person who owns the board you no longer want to follow to see the user's personal Pinterest page.

4. Click the Unfollow button for the given pinboard.

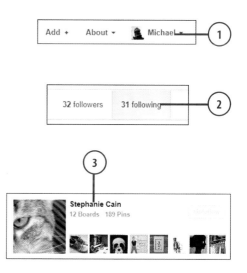

Pinboard   Pins

In this chapter, you learn how to create and manage topic-specific pinboards.

→ Understanding what pinboards are and how they work
→ Viewing pinboards and their contents
→ Creating new pinboards
→ Editing and deleting pinboards

Creating and Managing Pinboards

To post something you find interesting to Pinterest, you "pin" the item to a virtual corkboard of sorts called a *pinboard*. You can create as many pinboards as you like, each devoted to items related to a specific hobby or topic.

Understanding Pinboards

When you find an item you're interested in, you "pin" it to a virtual pinboard (sometimes just called a *board*) on the Pinterest site. What is a pinboard? Pinterest defines a board as "a set of pins." In practical terms, a pinboard, like a physical corkboard, is a place where you pin or post items of interest.

Each pinboard you create acts as a visual storehouse for the items you pin. Thumbnails for your last nine pins are displayed on the board's thumbnail; when you open the board, you see all the pins that you've posted to that board.

To best organize your pins, you should create pinboards devoted to the main topics or hobbies in which you're interested. Pinterest gets you started by creating five default boards for you, as follows:

- Favorite Places & Spaces
- For the Home
- Products I Love
- My Style
- Books Worth Reading

You're not limited to these five boards. You can rename or delete any of these default boards, or create any number of new boards devoted to your favorite topics. You can then add as many pins to each board as you like; there's no limit.

Each board is assigned to a specific category. When you create a new board, you can choose from the following Pinterest categories:

- Architecture
- Art
- Cars & Motorcycles
- Design
- DIY & Crafts
- Education
- Film, Music & Books
- Fitness
- Food & Drink
- Gardening
- Geek
- Hair & Beauty
- History
- Holidays
- Home Decor
- Humor
- Kids
- My Life
- Women's Apparel
- Men's Apparel
- Outdoors
- People
- Pets
- Photography
- Print & Posters
- Products
- Science & Nature
- Sports
- Technology
- Travel & Places
- Weddings & Events
- Other

When a board has been assigned to a category, users browsing Pinterest by category can then see this board.

Viewing Pinboards

Pinboards are where you and your friends post and store the items you find interesting. A user's boards are displayed on his or her personal Pinterest page.

Viewing Friends' Pinboards

A user's presence on Pinterest is defined by his or her pinboards and the pins posted there. To view a friend's pinboards and their contents, follow these steps:

1. Click the friend's name anywhere on the Pinterest site to see the friend's personal Pinterest page with thumbnails of all her pinboards.

Finding Users

You can find your Pinterest friends by using the search box at the top of every Pinterest page.

2. Click a board's thumbnail image to open it. The pins for the selected board display. Each pin consists of the pinned image, descriptive text (supplied by the user who pinned the item), and the URL for the website where this image was found.

3. Click any pin to visit the original page for the image.

Categorizing Boards

If a user has not yet assigned a category for a given pinboard, you see a "Help *user* categorize this board!" message at the top of the pinboard page. If you want to do this, select a category from the pull-down list.

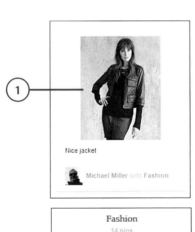

Nice jacket

Michael Miller onto Fashion

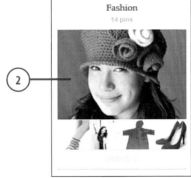

Fashion
14 pins

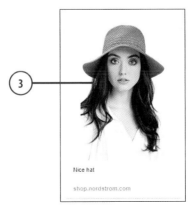

Nice hat

shop.nordstrom.com

Viewing Your Pinboards

You can also view your own pinboards on the Pinterest site.

1. Mouse over your name in the top-right corner of any Pinterest page.

2. Select Boards from the drop-down menu to see your personal Pinterest page, with thumbnails of all your pinboards.

3. Click a board's thumbnail image to view all the contents of a given pinboard.

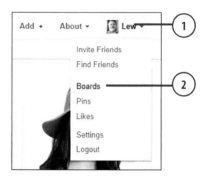

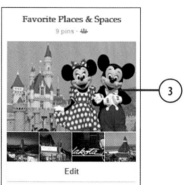

Creating New Pinboards

As previously noted, Pinterest creates five default pinboards when you first create your account. You can create additional boards if you like, to better match your own hobbies and interests.

Creating a Pinboard

You can create as many pinboards as you like.

1. Click Add+ on the Pinterest menu bar.

2. Click Create a Board in the Add panel.

3. Enter the name for the new board into the Board Name box in the Create a Board panel.

4. Pull down the Board Category list and select a category for this board.

5. Go to the Who Can Pin? section and, unless you plan to create a collaborative board, select the Just Me option.

6. Click the red Create Board button. Pinterest now creates the board and displays the page for this board (it's currently empty).

Collaborative Boards

Pinterest also lets you create collaborative pinboards. Learn more in Chapter 17, "Using Pinterest for Sharing and Collaboration."

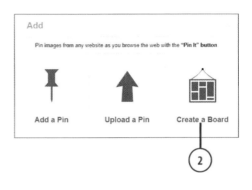

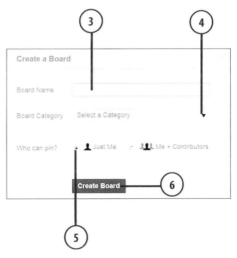

Editing and Deleting Pinboards

At any time you can rearrange, rename, or delete any of your pinboards. You can also delete individual pins from a given pinboard.

>>>step-by-step

Rearranging Pinboards

Your friends see the boards on your personal page in the order you designate. To rearrange your pinboards, follow these steps:

1.   Mouse over your name in the top-right corner of any Pinterest page.

2.   Select Boards from the drop-down menu.

3.   When your personal Pinterest page appears, click the Rearrange Boards button. The page opens for editing.

4.   Use your mouse to drag any board to a new position; your cursor changes to a four-sided arrow.

5.   Click the red checkmark button when done.

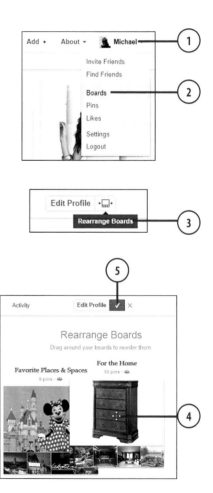

Renaming a Pinboard

Over time you might find that the contents of a particular board are not reflected in the board's name. In this instance, you can rename the pinboard.

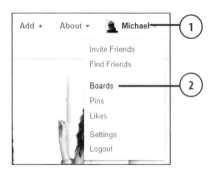

1. Mouse over your name in the top-right corner of any Pinterest page.

2. Select Boards from the drop-down menu. Your personal Pinterest page displays.

3. Click the Edit button for the pinboard you want to rename.

4. Type a new name into the Title box of the Edit Board page.

5. Click the red Save Settings button when done.

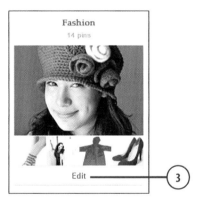

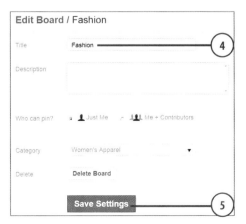

>>>step-by-step

Editing a Board's Description and Category

You can also add or edit a description for a given board and change the board's category.

1. Mouse over your name in the top-right corner of any Pinterest page.

2. Select Boards from the drop-down menu. Your personal Pinterest page displays.

3. Click the Edit button for the pin-board you want to edit.

4. Type a new description of the board into the Description box on the Edit Board page.

5. Pull down the Category list and make a new selection.

6. Click the red Save Settings button when done.

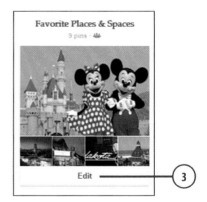

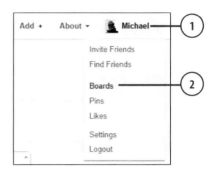

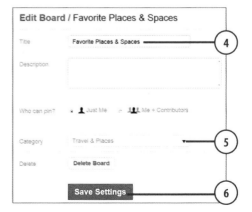

Deleting a Pinboard

If you find a particular pinboard falls into disuse, you might want to delete that board.

1. Mouse over your name in the top-right corner of any Pinterest page.

2. Select Boards from the drop-down menu. Your personal Pinterest page displays.

3. Click the Edit button for the pin-board you want to delete.

4. Click the Delete Board button on the Edit Board page.

5. Click the red Delete Board button in the confirmation box.

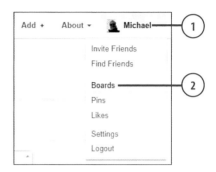

>>>step-by-step

Deleting Pins on a Pinboard

You can also edit the contents of any given board by deleting any items pinned to it.

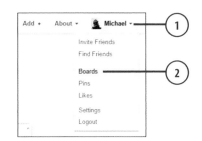

1. Mouse over your name in the top-right corner of any Pinterest page.

2. Select Boards from the drop-down menu. Your personal Pinterest page displays.

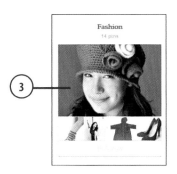

3. Click the thumbnail image for the given board. The pinboard's page displays.

4. Mouse over the item you want to delete and then click the Edit button for that item.

5. Click the Delete Pin button on the Edit Pin page.

6. Click the red Delete Pin button in the confirmation box.

Editing Pins

You can also use the Edit Pin page to edit an item's description and web link, as well as change to which it is pinned.

Selecting a Cover for a Pinboard

You can select which pin you want to be the cover picture at the top of the pinboard box. This way you can set a particular image to be the primary image for that board.

1. Mouse over your name in the top right corner of any Pinterest page.

2. Select Boards from the dropdown menu. Your personal Pinterest page displays.

3. Mouse over the board you wish to edit and click the Edit Board Cover button. You now see a panel that displays all the images for the pins on this board.

4. Click the right and left arrow buttons to scroll through the pinned images until you find the one you want to use as the cover.

5. Click and drag the image to crop it to fit in the designated space; the cursor changes to a four-sided arrow when you're repositioning the image.

6. Click the red Set Cover button when done.

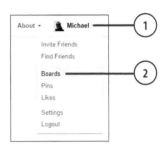

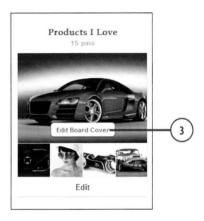

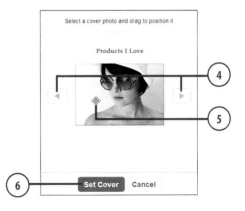

Image URL

Pinned image

Select pinboard

Pin description

In this chapter, you learn how to pin items to your boards on the Pinterest site.

- → Understanding how pins work
- → Pinning an item from the Pinterest website
- → Pinning an item using the Pin It button
- → Pinning an item you upload from your computer

6

Pinning to Pinterest

Pinterest is all about pinning items of interest—hence the name, a combination of "pin" and "interest." Pinterest's social sharing is based on the concept of pinning images and videos to your pinboards and then letting your friends visually browse the items you've pinned.

To fully participate in the Pinterest community, then, you have to learn how to pin items to your pinboards. There are a number of ways to do this.

Understanding Pins

What is a pin? In the world of Pinterest, a pin is an item that you've added to one of your personal pinboards. A pin can be an image or video you've found on another website or one that you've uploaded from your own computer.

Pins that you add from other websites become live links back to the image's original web page. Any user clicking this type of pin is taken to the web page where you found that particular item.

Each pin is accompanied by a short text description that you add. The text description can be up to 500 characters in length and is mandatory; you can't pin an image without a little text describing it.

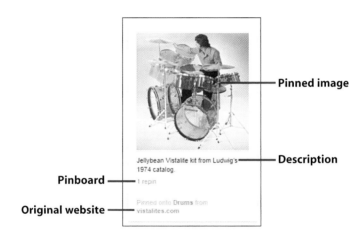

You pin your content (image, video, and so on) to a specific pinboard you've created. Although a pin can only be added to a single pinboard, you can move pins from one board to another, if you initially pinned them to the wrong board, or just decide it belongs on another board.

Pinning from the Pinterest Site

The simplest (but not necessarily the easiest) way to create a pin is from the Pinterest site. You can also install a Pin It button in your web browser or upload an image to pin, but those all require additional steps.

>>>step-by-step
Creating a Pin

To pin an item while you're using the Pinterest website, you need to know the address (URL) of the web page you want to pin. With that URL in hand, follow these steps:

1. Click Add+ on the Pinterest menu bar. The Add panel displays.

2. Click Add a Pin to view the Add a Pin panel.

3. Enter the URL of the page you want to pin.

4. Click the Find Images button. The Add a Pin panel now changes to display a slideshow of images found on the selected web page.

5. Click the Next or Prev buttons to cycle through the images until you find the one you want to pin.

6. Pull down the pinboard list and select the board to which you'd like to pin this image.

7. Enter a short (500 characters or less) text description of or comment on this image into the Describe Your Pin box.

8. Click the red Pin It button.

9. The image you selected is pinned to the selected board and displayed onscreen. You can now edit the pin or share it via Facebook or Twitter.

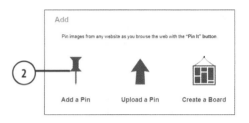

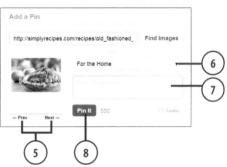

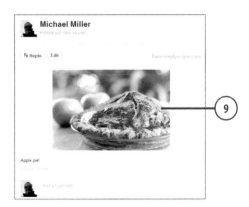

Pinning from Your Web Browser

The only problem with pinning an item from within Pinterest is that you have to know the precise URL of a web page beforehand. If you'd rather browse around the web for a bit before you decide to pin, it's more convenient to install a Pin It button in your web browser. You can then browse to a page you want to pin and click the Pin It button on your browser's toolbar to pin an image to your pinboard. The process of adding the Pin It button is different for different web browsers, so follow the directions for the browser you use.

Bookmarklet

The Pin It button is technically a bookmarklet, as it's a bookmark to a web page that performs a specified action.

Other Browsers

The following sections describe in detail how to add a Pin It button to the Internet Explorer and Google Chrome web browsers. You can also add Pin It buttons to other browsers, including Firefox, Safari, and Opera. Follow the instructions on the Pinterest site.

>>>*step-by-step*

Adding a Pin It Button to Internet Explorer

Before you can pin an item from Internet Explorer, you first have to install the Pin It button to the Favorites center.

1. In Internet Explorer, right-click in the window frame above the address bar and click Favorites Bar.

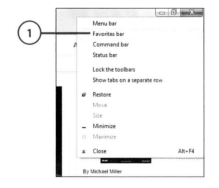

2. Log into your Pinterest account and mouse over About in the Pinterest menu bar.

3. Select Pin It Button from the drop-down menu. The Goodies page displays.

4. Right-click the Pin It button in the middle of the web page and select Add to Favorites.

5. When the Add to Favorites dialog box appears, make sure that Pin It is entered into the Name box.

6. Pull down the Create In list and select Favorites Bar.

7. Click the Add button.

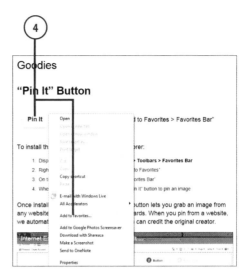

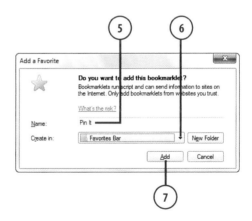

>>>*step-by-step*

Adding a Pin It Button to Google Chrome

Follow these steps to install the Pin It button in the Google Chrome browser:

1. In Google Chrome, click the Wrench icon in your browser and select Bookmarks.

2. Check Show Bookmarks Bar.

3. Log into your Pinterest account and mouse over About in the Pinterest menu bar.

4. Select Pin It Button from the drop-down menu.

5. Drag the Pin It button in the middle of the page to the desired position on the Bookmarks bar.

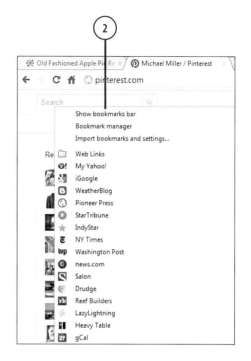

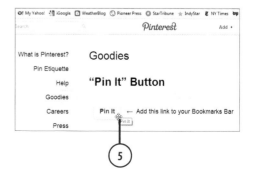

Pinning with the Pin It Button

After you've installed the Pin It button to your browser's Favorites or Bookmarks bar, adding a new pin is as easy as clicking that button.

1. Use your web browser to browse to the web page that contains the image you want to pin.

2. Click the Pin It button in your browser's Favorites or Bookmarks bar. Pinterest displays a page of images from the selected web page.

3. Mouse over a given image to display the Pin This button for that image.

4. Click the Pin This button for the image you want to pin. The Create Pin dialog box displays.

5. Pull down the pinboard list and select the board you want to pin to.

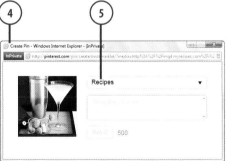

6. Enter a short (500 characters or less) text description into the Describe Your Pin box.

7. Click the red Pin It button.

8. Click the See Your Pin button to view the pin on Pinterest, or click Tweet This Pin to post this pin to Twitter.

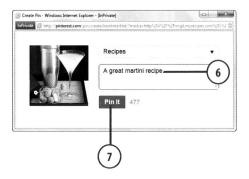

ADDING A PRICE

Many people pin items that would make good gifts, or that they might like to purchase in the future. In these instances, you might want to add the item's price to the pin's description. To do this, type the $ or £ symbol followed by the item's price. This lets other users see your pin when they're searching for an item by price point.

Uploading a Pin from Your Computer

The third way to pin an item is to upload an image from your computer to the Pinterest site. You can upload your pictures one at a time to the Pinterest site and have them appear alongside the web page images you pin.

>>>step-by-step

Uploading an Image to Pin

Follow these steps:

1. Click Add+ on the Pinterest menu bar.

2. Click Upload a Pin in the Add panel. The Upload a Pin panel displays.

3. Click the Browse or Choose File button. The Choose File to Upload or Open dialog box displays.

4. Navigate to and select the image file you want to upload and then click the Open button.

5. Pull down the pinboard list in the Upload a Pin panel and select the board to which you'd like to pin this image.

6. Enter a short (500 characters or less) text description of or comment on this image into the Describe Your Pin box.

7. Click the red Pin It button.

8. Pinterest uploads the image from your computer to the selected pinboard and displays it onscreen. You can now edit the pin or share it via Facebook or Twitter.

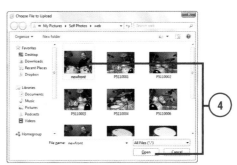

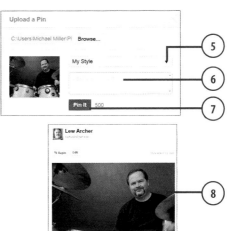

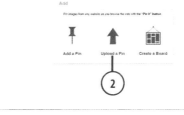

Playing a
pinned—
video

In this chapter, you learn how to post and play videos on Pinterest.

→ Understanding Pinterest's video pins
→ Pinning videos from YouTube
→ Finding videos on Pinterest
→ Playing pinned videos

Pinning and Playing Videos

Pinterest started out as a social network for images. In August 2011, however, Pinterest added another interesting feature—the capability to pin and share videos found on the Web, which made pinning videos as easy as pinning images. Videos are also easy to play on the Pinterest site.

Understanding Video Pins

A video pin is much like a traditional image pin except you're pinning a video file instead of an image file. You find a video you'd like to share and then you pin it to one of your Pinterest boards, the same way you'd pin an image. It's as easy as that.

The one caveat, at this point in time, is that you can only pin videos found on the YouTube site. Given that YouTube hosts and serves close to half of all the videos on the web today, that gives you a lot of videos to choose from. (The next-largest site, China's Youku, only has a 2% market share.) Still, don't expect to be able to pin any videos you find on Facebook or other non-YouTube sites.

Watching a pinned video on Pinterest is as easy as clicking the video thumbnail. The video opens in a larger viewing panel, and you can control playback using the standard YouTube video transport controls—as well as repin, like, and comment on the video you're viewing.

Pinning a Video

As noted, you can pin any public video you find on YouTube. You can't (as yet) pin videos from other websites.

>>>step-by-step

How to Pin a YouTube Video

The easiest way to pin a video is by using the Pin It button installed on your browser's Favorites or Bookmarks bar.

1. Point your web browser to the YouTube website (www.youtube.com) and find the video you want to pin.

2. Click the Pin It button on your browser's Favorites or Bookmarks bar. Pinterest displays a page of thumbnails for all the videos and images on this page; the main video has a Play arrow superimposed on the thumbnail.

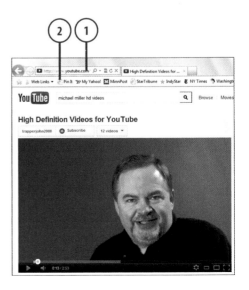

3. Mouse over this thumbnail to display the Pin This button and then click the button. The Create Pin dialog box displays.

4. Pull down the pinboard list and select the board to which you'd like to pin this video.

5. Enter a short (500 characters or less) text description of or comment on this image into the Describe Your Pin box.

6. Click the red Pin It button. The video is pinned to the selected board.

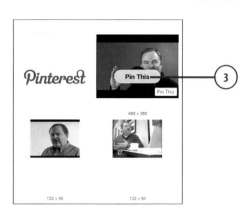

Viewing Pinned Videos

Viewing a video on Pinterest is as easy as clicking the video thumbnail—after you find the video, that is.

>>>*step-by-step*

Searching for Videos on Pinterest

There are two ways to find a video on the Pinterest site. You can search for videos or browse for them.

You search for videos the same way you search for other content on Pinterest.

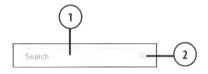

1. Enter one or more keywords that describe the video you're looking for into the search box at the top of any Pinterest page

2. Press the Enter key or click the magnifying glass button next to the search box. Pinterest returns a page of search results. Videos are indicated with a Play arrow super-imposed on the pin.

3. Click a video thumbnail to play the video.

Search Results

The results for any search you make can contain both images and videos. At present there is no way to filter your search to include videos only.

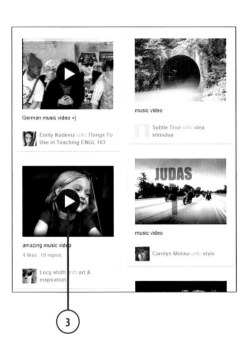

Browsing for Videos on Pinterest

Pinterest also enables you to browse all videos pinned to the site. You do this from Pinterest's home page.

1. Click the Pinterest logo at the top of any page to go to the home page.

2. Click the Videos link at the top of the page. Pinterest displays a variety of pinned videos with the most recent videos listed first.

3. Click a video thumbnail to play the video.

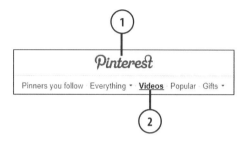

Viewing a Pinned Video

After you find a video that interests you, you can play the video directly from the Pinterest site.

1. Navigate to the video you want to play and click the video thumbnail. Pinterest displays a video playback pane.

2. The selected video begins playback automatically. Mouse over the video player to view the standard YouTube playback controls.

3. Click the Pause button to pause playback. To resume playback, click the Play button.

4. Click the Mute button to mute the sound. To raise or lower the sound, mouse over the Mute button to display and adjust the volume slider.

5. Use the time slider to move to another section of the video.

6. Click the Full Screen button to view the video in full screen mode. Press Esc to return to normal viewing mode.

7. Click the Change Quality button and make a selection to choose a higher resolution for playback.

8. Mouse over the video player and click the Repin button to repin the video.

9. Mouse over the video player and click the Like button to indicate that you like the video.

10. Enter a text message into the Add a Comment box beneath the video to comment on the pin and then press Return.

    To return to the previous page, click anywhere outside the video playback pane.

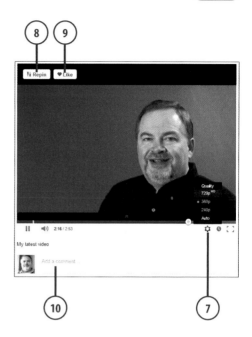

PLAYBACK RESOLUTION

Most pinned videos play at 360p resolution—that's 360 pixels high by 480 pixels wide. This resolution maximizes playback quality on slower Internet connections.

A majority of newer videos, however, are uploaded at higher resolutions, which look better when played on larger monitors. You can find videos at 480p, 720p, 1080p, the last two being full high-definition (HD) video. Changing playback resolution improves the quality of the picture, but it might result in unexpected pauses or stuttering playback because higher-resolution video requires more bandwidth to download and play back.

Pinboard

For the Home f Like

Michael Miller

63 followers. 9 pins

An inspirational garden.
mysite.verizon.net

Cool blue home theater
digital-global.org

Beautiful living room
socketsite.com

Multi-season garden.
hgtv.com

Nice bathroom
google.com

Stylish
1 repin

Pinned items

In this chapter, you learn how to find items to pin on Pinterest.

→ Understanding what people pin—and why
→ Pinning visually interesting items
→ Pinning inspirational and humorous items
→ Pinning gift ideas
→ Pinning bookmarks to web pages

Finding Interesting Things to Pin

Now that you know how to pin items on Pinterest, what kinds of items should you pin? Finding interesting things to pin is both fun and challenging; different people have different tastes and needs.

What—and Why—Do People Pin on Pinterest?

The rapid and relatively widespread appeal of Pinterest has everyone asking—why? That is, why do so many people use Pinterest, and what do they use it for?

It's all a matter of deciding what to pin. Although you can pretty much pin anything you like (within the constraints of acceptable content), you probably want to confine your pins those topic areas of most interest to you and your friends.

There is a dichotomy here. Some people pin items that are of interest to themselves in some fashion. They use Pinterest as kind of an online bookmarking system, much like the bookmarks or favorites you have in your web browser, but more visual. These people use Pinterest to store images of items they want to return to or revisit at a later date, for whatever reason.

Other people view Pinterest as a social network, much like Facebook, where they pin items they think will be of interest to their friends and followers. The goal here is not to use Pinterest to collect items for your personal use, but rather to share items that you think your friends will find interesting or useful.

As far as where to start, there's value in examining the five pinboards that Pinterest automatically creates for all new users. These default boards represent some of the most common interests of Pinterest users.

First up is Favorite Places & Spaces. Here you can pin pictures of places you've visited or would like to travel to, the city where you live or cities where you used to live, great-looking homes and rooms, landscapes and gardens that catch your fancy, that sort of thing. For example, if you've recently traveled to Paris, you might upload some of your vacation pics, or pin images of the City of Lights from other websites.

The second board is called For the Home, and this pinboard is designed to hold pins about home décor, accessories, landscaping, and other home-based projects. You can pin to this board pictures of room designs you'd like to implement, home furnishings and furniture you'd like to buy, DIY projects you might like to do some day, and the like. For example, you might head to the Ikea website and pin images of that new kitchen table you'd like to have.

Next is the Products I Love board, which is kind of a catch-all for items you think are cool or would like to purchase (or have given to you). You can pin virtually anything to this board, either for your own edification or as reminders to others when gift-giving time comes along. For example, if you're a big fan of Starbucks, you might pin an image of your favorite drink or coffee blend.

My Style is a board devoted to fashion and clothing. Here you pin pictures of fashionable dresses, loungewear, coats, sweaters, purses, you name it—items you like to wear or would like to wear. For example, if you're into exercising, you might pin images of this season's hottest exercise outfits.

The final board, Books Worth Reading, is where you let your friends know what you're reading or have read. Pin cover images of your favorite or most recently read books, and thus use Pinterest to share those titles you like. For example, if you're a devoted reader of the *Harry Potter* books, you might go to Amazon and pin images of the book covers you find there.

Now, these five boards are only a start. You'll end up creating a variety of boards that best match your own interests and activities—and it's those interests and activities that you'll be pinning about. Pin items you find interesting, useful, inspiring, beautiful, or humorous.

Of course, if you're pinning items to share with those that follow you, make sure your pins are interesting, useful, and so on to your friends and family, too.

In this fashion, think of Pinterest as a kind of visual scrapbook; pin the same sorts of images you'd include in a scrapbook to share with your friends.

Pinning Visually Interesting Items

Probably the first thing to keep in mind when you're looking for items to pin is that Pinterest is a visual social network. That is, you don't write about things, you show them to your friends. It's the old-picture-is-worth-a-thousand-words deal; the comments you add are much less important than the images you choose to pin.

This means that you always have to be on the lookout for visually interesting items. You can't pin text (unless it's represented graphically—more on this in a moment); you have to pin pictures, and the more attractive the picture, the better.

Take into account the typical size of a pinned image on the Pinterest site, and choose your images accordingly. In general, images of a single item against a plain background work better than images with multiple items against a more cluttered background. When it comes to the subject of a picture, bigger and bolder is always better.

You also want the image you choose to best represent the web page it links back to. For example, if you're pinning about a key lime pie recipe, pick a mouth-watering image of a finished pie, which should then link back to the web page that hosts the recipe for the pie.

Terrific key lime pie recipe!

tasteofhome.com

This brings us to the next point, that you shouldn't expect the image to carry the entire load. In the case of a food recipe, you really can't pin the recipe itself; an image is not a set of step-by-step instructions, and the limited accompanying text (500 characters or less) simply doesn't give you enough room for recipe details. Remember that your pins are clickable, and let the original web page do the heavy lifting for you.

It's Not All Good

One might think, given Pinterest's visual nature, that many folks would use the site to pin what some might refer to as "adult images." Indeed, one could imagine Pinterest becoming a mass repository for pins of images that might be labeled various degrees of obscene.

Fortunately, Pinterest management views its site as family friendly; the site's terms of service specifically bans nudity and obscene content. However, Pinterest has no content filters in place to identify prurient content. Instead, it relies on its users to report inappropriate images—and the user community takes this obligation seriously.

If you see an image on Pinterest that offends you, you can report it by clicking the thumbnail image to go to the detailed pin page. From there, click the Report Pin button and then select the reason you're reporting it—probably Nudity or Pornography. When Pinterest receives your report, this particular pin is automatically removed from general views (such as the Everything feed), but remains on the poster's personal pinboard. When Pinterest staff reviews the report, they can then choose to completely remove the pin from the site. That's if the pin is found to violate Pinterest's terms of service, of course; if the staff disagrees with the complaining user, the pin remains.

Of course, obscenity is the eye of the beholder, and what some people regard as smut others call art. If you don't believe me, check out Pinterest's Art or Porn board (www.pinterest.com/source/art-or-porn.com/), which hosts images that could fall into one or the other camp. Deciding what is appropriate or not becomes increasingly difficult when you're talking about women's fashion photography, especially the lingerie area. (The general photography area is also tricky.) It's tough to draw the line, sometimes, but Pinterest tries.

Pinning Text, Visually

Some users like to pin inspirational or humorous messages, much like the "fortunes" you find in Chinese fortune cookies. Because the message itself is decidedly non-visual (it's a collection of words, not an image), you have to turn the words into an image. To that end, several websites offer these types of messages in image format; you can then pin the image to your board, which delivers the message visually.

Some of these message images sites include the following:

- Cherry Bam (www.cherrybam.com/funny-quotes.php)

- Free Funny Pixs (www.freefunnypixs.com)

- My Funny World (myfunnyworld.net/category/funny-jokes-quotes)

- SomeEcards (www.someecards.com)

- The Chive (www.thechive.com)

- ThinkNice (www.thinknice.com/cute-pin-up-quotes/)

Pinning Inspirational Items

Much of the text-as-image pins convey inspirational messages. But there's another kind of inspiration for which Pinterest is uniquely suited—providing inspiration for your future projects.

Using Pinterest in this fashion is like thumbing through home or fashion magazines and ripping out pages that interest you. Instead of stuffing printed pages into some sort of notebook for future use, you instead pin those pages (or the images on those pages) to a special Pinterest board. Then, when you need inspiration, all you need do is return to that board to visually thumb through the images.

What kind of inspirational items might you pin? Photographers might pin photos that inspire. Home designers (or anyone planning a home renovation project) might pin pictures of room layouts they like. Landscape designers or home gardeners might pin pictures of landscapes or gardens that are appealing. Prospective brides might pin interesting wedding or bridal ideas. It's all a matter of finding images that inspire, and then pinning them for future reference.

An inspirational garden.

mysite.verizon.net

Where can you find images that inspire? It all depends. For inspiring fashions, checkout fashion websites and online clothing retailers. For inspiring photographs, Flickr is always good. For inspiring home design, check out online home furnishing retailers and home décor websites. You get the picture.

Pinning Humorous Items

The "Pinning Text, Visually" section discusses how to pin text messages as images. This is a good way to pin not only inspiring messages, but also humorous messages. Everybody likes to share a good laugh, after all.

Imagine...

blippitt.com

The message images sites listed previously contain a good number of humorous messages you can pin. You might also want to check out sites that offer humorous images, such as

- Photobucket (www.photobucket.com/images/humor/)
- Uberhumor (www.uberhumor.com)
- EatLiver (www.eatliver.com)
- FailBlog (www.failblog.org)
- FunnyJunk (www.funnyjunk.com)

And, of course, don't forget the source of those funny LOL cats pics, I Can Has Cheezburger? (www.icanhascheezburger.com).

Pinning Lifestyle Items

Lots of users like to pin lifestyle-related items on their Pinterest boards. This can cover a lot of territory, from merchandise you'd like to buy to crafts you've made (or would like to make), from clothing and furniture to collectibles and hobbies, from pictures of famous people to pictures of your own family. In short, whatever suits your own lifestyle is prime for pinning.

A collectible Barbie doll.

hardtofindantiques.com

Where can you find lifestyle pictures? It depends on your lifestyle. Online retailers, whether Nordstrom's or Wal-Mart, feature pictures of all sorts of merchandise you can pin. Hobbyist sites offer photos from other hobbyists. If it's a website you frequent, chances are there are photos there you can pin.

You can also upload your own lifestyle photos to Pinterest. If you buy a fancy new car, upload a photo of it. If you're all dressed up for a night on the town, share your look by uploading a photo. If you've worked hard on a new crafts project, take a photo and upload it.

In short, look for where you learn and talk about lifestyle-related items (including in your own home), and pin the photos you find there.

Pinning Things You Want to Do—and Places You Want to Go

Back on the topic of inspirational items, many folks use Pinterest to pin ideas for things they want to do sometime in the future—or places they'd like to visit. Maybe you find a great recipe for beef stroganoff; pin a picture of the dish (and link to the recipe) to a Pinterest board for future use. Or perhaps there's a big DIY or crafts project that catches your eye; pin a picture of the project to Pinterest and refer to it when you have the time.

You can find these sorts of images in lots of places online. Pinnable recipes are best found at any number of recipe-related websites; you can go to your favorite crafts and DIY sites for photos of projects you'd like to pin.

Our dream Disney World vacation

blog.etravel.com

The same approach goes for upcoming vacations. Find a photo of a place to which you'd like to travel, and pin it to a "dream vacations" pinboard. For example, if you really want to take your kids to Disney World someday, pin a photo of the Magic Kingdom on your Pinterest board. You can find location and vacation photos on many sites across the Web; try looking at local chamber of commerce sites, travel sites, and websites for specific attractions.

Pinning Gift Ideas

Then there's the concept of using Pinterest to host your gift list. No matter what the occasion, Pinterest can not only store pictures of items you'd like to receive, but also helps serve them to those people who'll be buying the gifts.

For our wedding registry

conefivepottery.com

Take, for example, the concept of a Pinterest wedding registry. All you have to do is create a "wedding registry" pinboard and then visit those sites that sell the items you'd like to receive. Pin pictures of each item to the board and then share the board's URL with your family and wedding guests. Interested parties can click the picture of an item to be taken to the website selling that item. It's a win-win for everybody.

The same goes for gifts for other occasions. Pinterest can host your Christmas wish list or items you'd like to receive for your birthday. Children can even use it to pin pictures of the toys on their wish lists. It's useful for your friends and family, and fun to browse through on your own. Plus, you can add prices to your pins, so folks can know how much they need to spend on an item.

PRICING AN ITEM

To add a price to a potential gift item, type the $ or £ symbol followed by the item's price. Doing so gives potential gift givers an idea of whether or not a given item is in their price range.

BOOKMARKING WITH PINS

Many people use Pinterest to bookmark their favorite websites. This makes Pinterest kind of a web-based visual alternative to traditional browser bookmarks and favorites; instead of clicking on a button in your browser's Bookmarks or Favorites bar, you find the items' thumbnail in a Pinterest board and click that image to go to the destination website.

Some people like organizing their favorite websites visually. Pick a representative image from the site, something that visually reminds you of what the site is about and then pin that image to a pinboard. Create separate pinboards for different types of websites, if you like, and you're well on your way to visually organizing your favorite sites.

For example, you might create separate pinboards for news, shopping, cooking, and parenting sites. Pin links to your favorite sites in each category to the appropriate pinboard.

You can also use Pinterest to organize links and ideas for any business project on your agenda. Just create a pinboard for each project and then post image links to sites that contain the information you need to reference.

Using Pinterest in this fashion is certainly easier than saving shortcuts to your favorite web pages on your Windows or Mac desktop. It also makes it easier to find specific sites than using your browser's text-based Bookmarks or Favorites feature.

Click to like this pin

Click to repin

Got a little Cosby #sweater thing going here

etsy.com

Click to add a comment

In this chapter, you learn how to like, repin, and comment on pins, as well as include hashtags and mentions in your pins.

→ Liking a pin
→ Repinning a pin
→ Commenting on a pin
→ Hashtagging keywords
→ Mentioning other users

Liking, Repinning, and Commenting

Viewing pins from other Pinterest users can be both fun and inspiring. You're likely to find lots of pins you like, or that you'd like to comment on. You might even find some pins you'd like to pin to your own pinboards.

Fortunately, Pinterest lets you do all this.

Liking Pins You Like

If you find a pin that you particularly like, why not tell Pinterest about it? Well, you can, because Pinterest lets you "like" any individual pin, just by clicking a button.

Any item that you "like" is automatically added to the Likes section of your personal Pinterest page. Your "like" is also added to other users' "likes," and noted on this item's pin.

You Can't Like Yourself

You can like any pin you find on Pinterest—except for your own. You can only like pins from other users, not from yourself.

>>>step-by-step

Liking a Pin

When you find a pin you like, "liking" it is a matter of clicking a button.

1. Mouse over the pin you want to like.

2. Click the Like button.

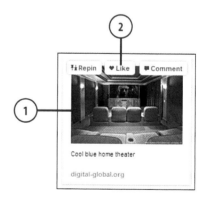

Viewing the Pins You Like

All the items you've liked appear in the Likes section of your personal Pinterest page. Follow these steps to view your likes—and "unlike" any item:

1. Mouse over your name in the Pinterest menu bar.

2. Click Likes from the drop-down menu. All the pins you've liked are displayed.

3. Mouse over a pin and click the Unlike button to remove an item.

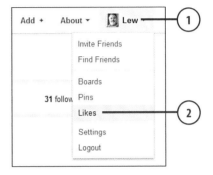

Repinning a Favorite Pin

Sometimes "liking" a pin isn't enough. Some pins are just so good you want to add them to your own pinboards—which you can do by *repinning* them.

Put simply, when you repin an item someone else previously pinned, you pin that item directly to one of your pinboards. The pin functions like any other pin, in that clicking it takes the user back to the page where the image originally appeared.

Pin Credit

When you repin an image, the user who originally created that pin receives credit for your repin.

Many Pinterest users find the most items to add to their own pinboards by repinning items from other users. In fact, more than 80% of all items on Pinterest are repins. You can repin an item from its thumbnail view or from its detailed pin page.

>>>*step-by-step*

Pinning an Item from Its Thumbnail

You can repin items you see when viewing pin thumbnails on any page on the Pinterest site.

1. Mouse over the pin you want to repin.

2. Click the Repin button to display the Repin panel.

3. Pull down the pinboard list and select which board you want to pin this item to.

4. Accept the previous user's description or add your own to the large text box.

5. Click the red Pin It button.

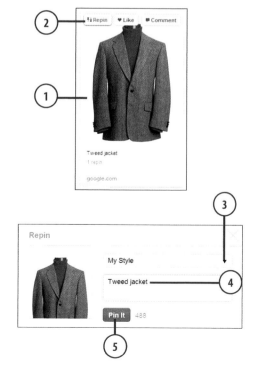

Pinning an Item from the Pin Page

You can also repin an item from its full-sized, detailed view.

1. Click the thumbnail image of the pin you want to repin to view the detailed pin panel.

2. Click the Repin button and the Repin panel displays.

3. Pull down the pinboard list and select which board you want to pin this item to.

4. Accept the previous user's description or add your own to the large text box.

5. Click the red Pin It button.

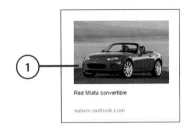

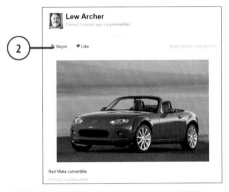

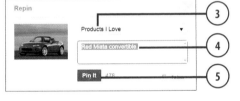

REPINNING VERSUS LIKING

Repinning is subtly differing from liking a pin. Liking a pin adds the pin your profile's Likes section, but does not add it to any of your pinboards. Repinning an item, in contrast, does add the item to your pinboard. In addition, you can edit the description of a repin, which you can't do when you merely like an item.

Commenting on a Pin

Another way to appreciate a pin you particularly like is to comment on it—
that is, to leave your written thoughts for the person who pinned the item.
Comments appear under the pinned image in both thumbnail and detailed
views.

You can comment on a pin in either view.

>>>*step-by-step*

Leaving a Comment in Thumbnail View

To leave a comment on a pinned item in
thumbnail view, follow these steps:

1. Mouse over the pin on which you
   want to comment.

2. Click the Comment button to
   open a comment box under the
   thumbnail image.

3. Type your comments into the
   comment box.

4. Click the Comment button to post
   your comment.

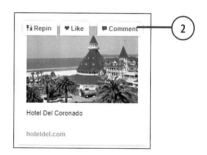

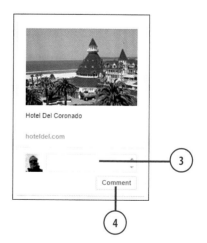

Leaving a Comment on the Pin Page

You can also make comments when you're viewing a pin in full-size view.

1. Click the thumbnail image of the pin on which you want to comment to view the detailed pin panel.

2. Enter your comments into the Add a Comment box beneath the main image.

3. Click the Post Comment button when done.

A great martini recipe.

myrecipes.com

Using Hashtags and Mentions

Sometimes you want others to see or find a pin you've made. You do this by adding *hashtags* and *mentions* in your pin's description.

>>>step-by-step

Adding a Hashtag to a Pin

To make sure a pin shows up when others search for a particular keyword, you can add a hashtag to the pin's description. A hashtag is simply a word with a number sign (#) in front of it. The hashtag identifies or "tags" the word as a searchable keyword.

For example, if you're pinning a picture of a dress, you might create the hashtag **#dress**. If you're pinning a picture of a leather jacket, you might create the hashtag **#leatherjacket**—note that you need to combine the two words to create a single hashtag.

Words Only
A hashtag applies only to the following word; the hashtag ends at the first space after the word. Thus you cannot tag multiple-word phrases, unless you run the words together—which is accepted style.

To add a hashtag to a pin's description, follow these steps:

1. Create a pin as normal.

2. In the description box, enter the # symbol, followed immediately by the keyword you want to tag.

3. Finish creating the pin as normal and then click the red Pin it button.

>>>step-by-step

Viewing Similar Pins via Hashtag

In practice, hashtags in a pin's description are clickable. The hashtagged word appears as bold text, and an underline appears when you mouse over the tag. When you click a hashtag, Pinterest displays other pins that include the same keyword.

To view other similar pins, follow these steps:

1. View the tag and look for a bold word preceded by the # sign. This is the hashtag. Click it.

2. Pinterest displays a page of pins that include this word in the item's description. Click a pin to view more details.

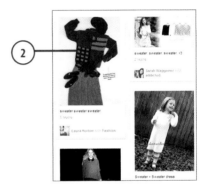

Recommending a Pin to Another User

If you want to recommend a pin to another user, you can "mention" that person in the pin's description. When you mention a person this way, she receives an email from Pinterest notifying her about and linking to the pin.

Only Mention People You Follow
Pinterest only lets you mention users that you formally follow.

To mention a user in a pin's description, follow these steps:

1. Create a pin as normal and enter the pin's description.

2. Enter the @ symbol, followed immediately by the person's username or email address, like this: **@melanie**. Pinterest displays potential matches from the people you follow.

3. Click the person you want to mention and finish creating the pin as normal.

Click to view
and edit
pinboards

Click to
view
likes

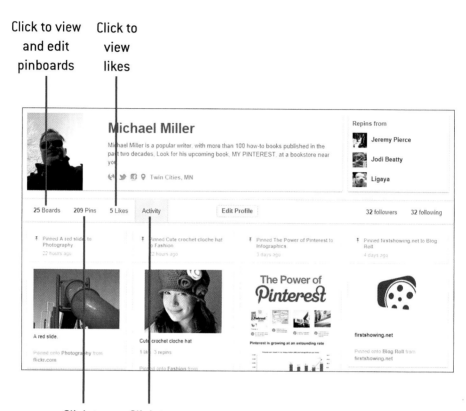

Michael Miller

Michael Miller is a popular writer, with more than 100 how-to books published in the past two decades. Look for his upcoming book, MY PINTEREST, at a bookstore near you.

Twin Cities, MN

Repins from

Jeremy Pierce

Jodi Beatty

Ligaya

25 Boards   209 Pins   5 Likes   Activity   Edit Profile   32 followers   32 following

Pinned A red slide to Photography
22 hours ago

Pinned Cute crochet cloche hat to Fashion
22 hours ago

Pinned The Power of Pinterest to Infographics
3 days ago

Pinned firstshowing.net to Blog Roll
4 days ago

A red slide.

Pinned onto Photography from flickr.com

Cute crochet cloche hat

1 like 3 repins

Pinned onto Fashion from

The Power of Pinterest

Pinterest is growing at an astounding rate

firstshowing.net

Pinned onto Blog Roll from firstshowing.net

Click to
view and
edit pins

Click to
view
recent
activity

→ Viewing your boards, pins, and likes

→ Editing your pins

→ Deleting pins

Viewing and Editing Your Pinterest Activity

When you pin an item to Pinterest, it's not set in stone. If you want, you can edit the description of any pin you've made, as well as delete those pins you no longer need or want others to see.

Viewing Your Pinterest Activity

Let's start by viewing all of your activity on the Pinterest site. Pinterest tracks the boards you create, the pins you make, and the pins that you "like" (by clicking that item's Like button).

>>>step-by-step

Viewing Your Boards

To view all your Pinterest boards and their contents, follow these steps:

1. Mouse over your name in the Pinterest menu bar.

2. Click Boards from the drop-down menu. Pinterest displays all your pinboards in thumbnail view.

3. Click a board to view its full page.

4. The top of the board page, under the board name, displays how many people are following this board and how many pins you've made to it.

5. Click a pin to view any individual pin on this board.

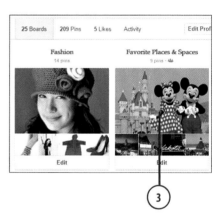

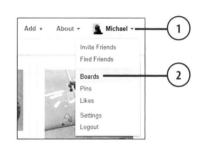

Viewing Your Pins

You can display the pins made to a given pinboard, as just explained, or you can view a list of all the pins you've made to Pinterest. Follow these steps:

1. Mouse over your name in the Pinterest menu bar.

2. Select Pins from the drop-down menu.

3. Your pins are displayed in the main part of the page, most recent first. Click a pin to view more detail.

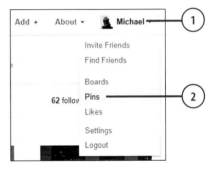

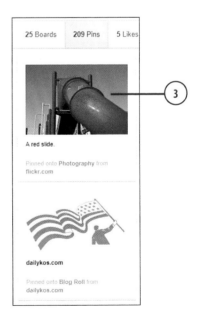

Viewing Your Likes

Pinterest also lets you view pins made by other users that you've previously "liked." To view these liked pins, follow these steps:

1. Mouse over your name in the Pinterest menu bar.

2. Select Likes from the drop-down menu to view the Likes page and the pins you've liked.

3. Click a pin's thumbnail image to view the details of the pin.

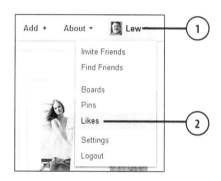

Viewing Stats

Your personal statistics—how many people are following you, as well as how many people you're following—are displayed at the top of the left sidebar on the Boards, Pins, and Likes pages, just below your name. Click Followers to see the people who are following you; click Following to see the people (and boards) that you're following.

Editing and Deleting Pins

A pin is not forever. You can, at any time, edit the information you've added to a pin or delete a pin entirely.

>>>step-by-step

Editing Information About a Pin

There are two ways to edit a pin. You can mouse over a pin in thumbnail view and click the Edit button, or you can open the pin's detail view and click the Edit button on that page. This task covers the first method; after the initial step, everything else is the same for the two methods.

Follow these steps to edit a pin from its thumbnail view:

1. Mouse over the pin you want to edit.

2. Click the Edit button to view the Edit Pin page.

3. Edit the text in the Description box.

4. Edit the URL in the Link box if you need to change the web address of the page to which the pin points.

5. Pull down the Board list and click the name of the new board if you want to move the pin to a different pinboard.

6. Click the red Save Pin button when done.

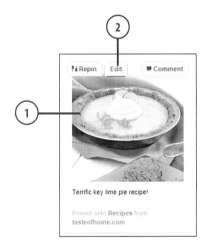

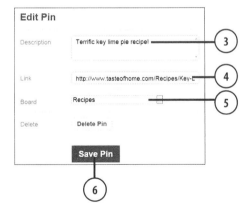

>>>step-by-step

Deleting a Pin

If you use pins as personal bookmarks, you might find that you no longer have need for a given pin. Likewise, you might have pinned something to share with your friends that you no longer want to share. In either instance, it's easy to delete an individual pin.

1. Mouse over the pin you want to delete.

2. Click the Edit button to view the Edit Pin page.

3. Click the Delete Pin button.

4. Click the red Delete Pin button.

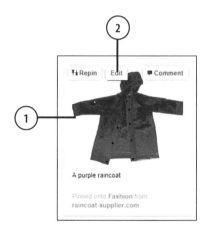

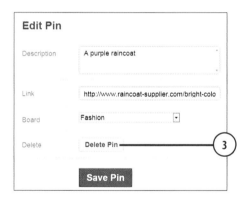

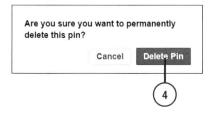

It's Not All Good

NO UNDELETE

When you delete a pin, it's permanently deleted; there's no way to restore it to your pinboard. If you later change your mind and want to restore the pin, you have to start from scratch and re-create it as a new pin.

Pinterest activity on Facebook Timeline

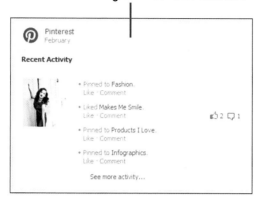

In this chapter, you learn how to share your favorite pins via Facebook, Twitter, and email—and by embedding them on your blog or web page.

→ Sharing pins via Facebook

→ Sharing pins via Twitter

→ Sharing Pins via email

→ Embedding pins on a blog or web page

Sharing Pins to Facebook and Twitter

Pinterest is a social network, which means it's all about sharing things you like with your friends and family. But you're not limited to sharing items only on the Pinterest site; you can also share your pins on Facebook and Twitter and via email. You can even embed a pin on your own blog or web page!

Sharing Pins via Facebook

If you belong to more than one social network, you don't necessarily want to re-create the same post multiple times. It's a lot more convenient if you can make a single post and then have it sent to all your social networks.

Facebook is the largest social network today, so it's convenient that you can link your Pinterest account to your Facebook account. Once linked, you can invite your Facebook friends to join you on Pinterest, as well as post your favorite Pins to your Facebook news feed.

>>>step-by-step

Linking Your Pinterest and Facebook Accounts

The first step in getting Pinterest and Facebook to work together is to link your two accounts.

1. Mouse over your name in the Pinterest menu bar.

2. Click Settings from the drop-down menu to view the Edit Profile page.

3. Scroll down to the Facebook section and click "on" the Link to Facebook item. The Facebook Login dialog box displays.

4. Enter your Facebook email address into the Email box.

5. Enter your Facebook password into the Password box.

6. Click the Log In button. The Request for Permission dialog box displays.

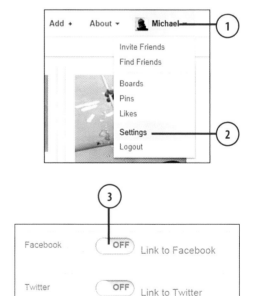

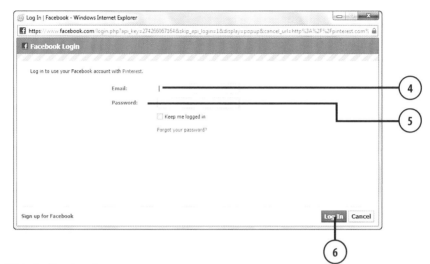

7. Click the Use App button.

8. Return to the Pinterest Edit Profile page and click the red Save Profile button at the bottom.

>>>step-by-step

Adding Pinterest to Your Facebook Timeline

You can also opt to add a Pinterest item to your Facebook Timeline, as well as post any new pins you make to your Facebook news feed.

1. Mouse over your name in the Pinterest menu bar.

2. Click Settings from the drop-down menu to view the Edit Profile page.

3. Scroll down to the Facebook section and click "on" the Add Pinterest to Facebook Timeline item. The Request for Permission dialog box displays.

4. Click the Add to Facebook button.

5. Return to the Pinterest Edit Profile page and click the red Save Profile button at the bottom.

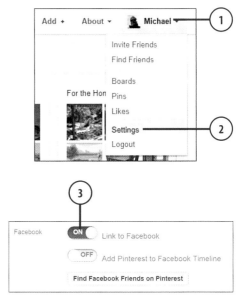

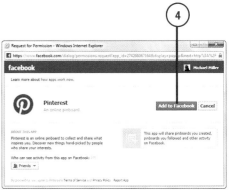

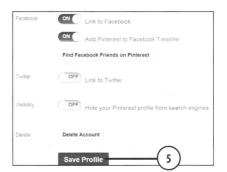

Liking a Pin on Facebook

You can also post any pin you find on the Pinterest site, whether posted by you or by anyone else, to Facebook. All you have to do is tell Facebook that you "like" the pin. The pin now appears as a status update in your Facebook news feed.

Different Likes

Don't confuse a Facebook "like" with a Pinterest "like." Clicking the Facebook Like button shares a pin with your Facebook friends; clicking the Pinterest Like button adds the pin to your Pinterest Like list.

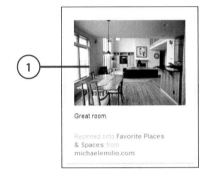

Great room.

Repinned onto Favorite Places & Spaces from michaelemilio.com

Here's how to do it:

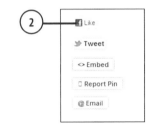

1. Find the pin you want to share and then click it. The detailed pin panel displays.

2. Click the Facebook Like button to the right of the image.

LIKING A PINBOARD

You can also "like" an entire pinboard to Facebook. Just navigate to the pinboard page and click the Facebook Like button at the top.

Likewise, you can "like" any person on Pinterest to Facebook. Just navigate to that person's Pinterest page and click the Facebook Like button in the left sidebar under that person's profile picture.

Sharing Pins via Twitter

Just as you can link your Pinterest account to your Facebook account, you can also link your Pinterest account to your Twitter account, if you have one. This enables you to share the pins you make with your Twitter followers, by tweeting about them.

>>>*step-by-step*

Linking Your Pinterest and Twitter Accounts

Before you can tweet your pins, you have to link your Pinterest and Twitter accounts.

1. Mouse over your name in the Pinterest menu bar.

2. Click Settings from the drop-down menu to view the Edit Profile page.

3. Scroll down to the Twitter section and click "on" the Link to Twitter item. The Authorize Pinterest to Use Your Account? dialog box displays.

4. Enter your email address or Twitter username into the Username or Email box.

5. Enter your Twitter password into the Password box.

6. Click the Sign In button.

7. Return to the Pinterest Edit Profile page and click the red Save Profile button.

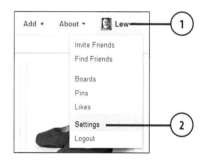

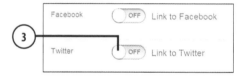

Tweeting a New Pin to Twitter

After you've linked your two accounts, you can send any new pin you create to Twitter. The pin appears as a regular Twitter tweet with a link back to the pin on the Pinterest site.

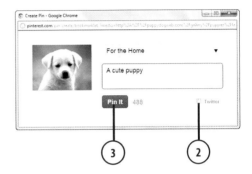

1. Create a pin as normal.

2. Check the Twitter box in the Create Pin dialog box.

3. Click the red Pin It button.

ANOTHER WAY TO TWEET

You can also tweet a pin after you've clicked the Pin It button. When the Success! dialog box appears, click the Tweet Your Pin button. If you're not currently signed into Twitter, you're prompted to enter your username and password. When you see the What's Happening? dialog box, edit the text and click the Tweet button.

Tweeting an Existing Pin

You're not limited to tweeting new pins you make. You can also tweet about an existing pin—either one you posted or one posted by another Pinterest user.

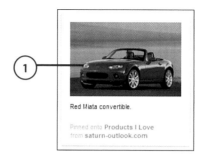

1. Find the pin you want to tweet about and click it. The detailed pin panel displays.

2. Click the Tweet button to the right of the image to view the Share a Link on Twitter dialog box.

3. Edit the text as you'd like.

4. Click the Tweet button.

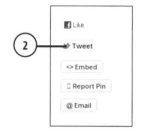

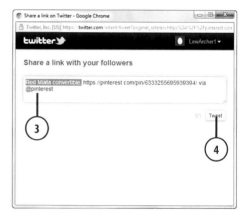

Sharing Pins with Non-Pinterest Users via Email

You can also use email share a favorite pin with friends who are not on Facebook or Twitter.

Sharing a Pin via Email

Pinterest lets you share any pin with anyone on the Internet, via email.

1. Find the pin you want to share and click it. The detailed pin panel displays.

2. Click the @Email button to the right of the image to view the Email This Pin dialog box.

3. Enter the recipient's name in the Recipient Name box.

4. Enter the recipient's email address into the Recipient Email box.

5. Enter an optional accompanying message into the Message box.

6. Click the Send Email button. The recipient receives an email containing your text message and a link to the pin on the Pinterest site.

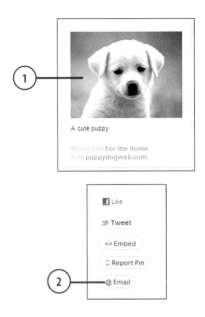

A cute puppy

Pinned onto For the Home
from puppydogweb.com

- Like
- Tweet
- <> Embed
- Report Pin
- @ Email

Email This Pin

Recipient Name —— ③

Recipient Email —— ④

Message (optional) —— ⑤

Send Email

Email This Pin

Lew Archer

lewarcher2010@gmail.com

A very cute puppy for you.

Send Email —— ⑥

Don't post
inappropriate
content

→ Learn the right ways to pin

→ Discover how to pin items you create or sell

→ Find out what *not* to pin

Learning Pinterest Etiquette

It takes a bit of time to learn all the ins and outs of pinning items on Pinterest. What kinds of things should you pin—or not pin? Is it okay to repin an image you found in another pin? How much description do you need to provide for a pin? Can you create pins for your own crafts or products?

Yes, there is a certain etiquette to pinning—let's call it *pin-etiquette*. Follow these unstated rules, and you'll be a happy pinner with lots of happy followers.

The Right Ways to Pin

As you've learned throughout this book so far, it's relatively easy to pin an item to a Pinterest pinboard. But there's more to pinning than just finding an image you want to share. You need to do a few little things to ensure that others will get the most from the items you pin.

It's Okay to Repin

First of all, know that you're not limited to pinning items you find elsewhere on the Web. It's perfectly acceptable—actually, *encouraged*—to repin items you see from other Pinterest users.

You see, repinning is part of the sharing culture that defines Pinterest and other social networks. Repinning *is* sharing, and that's what Pinterest is all about. (In fact, more than 80% of all pins on Pinterest are repins.)

Click to repin

When you repin an item, you're telling the original pinner that you like something she posted, and you're stating your own fondness for that item. There's nothing wrong with letting another user do the finding; by taking advantage of the other user's work, you can quickly and easily find items to fill up your pinboards.

Always Pin from the Original Source

One of the most important things to do when pinning is to make sure that you're pinning an item from its original source. You don't want to pin—or repin—an item that accidentally or purposefully posted an image that was the property of another website.

This is an issue because you want to credit (and send traffic to) the original item's rightful owner. It's not good to pin an item that links to a third-party website, thus letting that site get all the traffic (and advertising revenue) from your Pinterest followers. You want to credit the original owner of that item, not a copycat.

As an example, let's say you find an interesting craft on a blog, and thus pin that item to one of your Pinterest boards. If that craft did not originate on that blog—that is, if the blogger had copied and pasted the image and text from its original source—then you're not giving credit where credit is due. The original source doesn't receive any attention, whereas the blogger who copied the item gets all the traffic and attention.

This is bad not only because it slights the original content provider, but also because you're sending your Pinterest followers to a site or blog that probably doesn't have the full content found on the original site. If it's a craft you've repinned, for example, the original site might offer additional crafts of various types, whereas the blog that copied the craft probably won't have anything else of interest.

This is why you want to credit and pin from the original source, if you can. Remember, many craftspeople, artisans, designers, and photographers make some or all of their money from the Internet. When used properly, Pinterest sends traffic and potential customers to these small businesspeople. If your pin doesn't link to the creator's site, however, you're taking food out of that person's mouth.

SOURCING REPINS

The problem of not crediting the original source is also an issue when you're repinning an item. You may innocently repin an item you find on Pinterest, without realizing that the person who created the original pin found it on a site that copied it from the original website or blog.

To that end, it's worth clicking through a pin of interest before you repin. Make sure, as much as you can, that the linked-to site is the creator of the item or image of interest. If, instead, you find that it's a copyrighted image copied from another site, then go to the original site and create a new pin from there.

Always Pin from a Blog Post's Permalink

You can find many interesting items to pin in the blogosphere. Blogging and pinning are complementary activities, and you'll find lots of pinned items that originated on one or another blog.

When you want to pin an item from a blog, there's a right way and a wrong way to do it. The right way is to pin to the permanent link (*permalink*) to the specific blog post. The wrong way is to pin to the blog's main URL.

When you pin to a post's permalink, people who click the pin always go to the specific blog post that contains the item of interest. On the other hand, if you link to the blog itself, someone clicking your pin will likely see the blog's most recent post, not the post you wanted to point to.

The challenge is finding the post's permalink. What you don't want to do is go to the main blog page, scroll through the posts until you find the one you want, and then click the Pin It button. This creates a pin to the main blog page, not to the individual post.

Click the post title to open the post page →

The permalink URL includes a slash and page name

Instead, click the title of the blog post to open that post in its own web page. You can then click the Pin It button from that page or copy the URL of that page. (The URL of the individual blog post page is the permalink.)

Permalinks

You can identify the permalink by the format of the web page address (URL). The blog's main URL is typically something simple, like this: **www.blogname.com**. The permalink for a particular article typically incorporates the main URL but adds more information after a slash mark, like this: **www.blogname.com/articlename**. If you're looking at a longer URL with a slash in it, that's probably the permalink.

Always Write a Good Description

A picture may be worth a thousand words, but that doesn't mean you shouldn't use any words at all. Although the images are integral to Pinterest's social sharing, the descriptions you add to each image increase the value of each item you pin.

The more information you can add to a pin, the more useful that pin is to others. Adding a one-word description like "great" or "cute" doesn't cut it. You need to add more value than that.

One reason to write longer descriptions is because that's how other users find your pins. Pinterest doesn't know what's in a given picture; there's no technology today that can derive content from an image. Instead, Pinterest relies on the text descriptions to determine what a given pin is about, and then match that pin to related searches. In other words, if you don't describe the item you're pinning, no one else will be able to find or view that pin.

The text that accompanies a pin can also provide information that supplements the image. For example, you might pin an image of a good-looking armoire. The pin's description could inform viewers where that armoire can be purchased, or where you found it, or, if it's a DIY project, how to build it.

Pin description —

The Hamlyn armoire at Ashley Furniture. Rich traditional style with a European flair. It has a rich medium brown finish over a cherry veneer, with antique bronze hardware. Dimensions are 40" W x 19" D x 50" H.

Michael Miller onto For the Home

Step-by-Step Instructions

Given Pinterest's 500-character limit, you won't always have room to provide full step-by-step instructions for DIY projects or recipes. You have to rely on the link to the original source to provide more detailed instructions, but you can still give your followers a hint of what's involved in the descriptive text.

In any case, try to avoid one- or two-word descriptions. Take the effort to write a sentence or two about what you're pinning; your followers will thank you for the information.

Always Use #Hashtags

Speaking of a pin's text description, remember that you can use hashtags to identify keywords for the items you pin. When you put the hashtag character (#) in front of a word, that word becomes clickable. When one of your followers clicks a hashtagged word, Pinterest displays a whole page of pins related to that word.

Hashtag

So, for example, if you create a pin for a picture of a cute puppy, hashtag the word "puppy," like this: **#puppy**. Anyone who clicks that word in your pin's description will be shown a bunch of puppy pins.

Always Be Nice

Here's one final tip to take in mind when you're pinning and repinning. Pinterest is a social community, and as such you need to play nice with the other people in the community. Some of Pinterest's users will share your tastes, some won't, but you need to be nice to everyone, whether your agree or disagree with what they pin. That means avoiding "flame wars" with other pinners, and being respectful in the comments you make.

Your time is too valuable to waste on negative comments and online arguments.

Pinning Your Own Stuff

You might have noticed that many Pinterest users pin personal photos and items they've created to their pinboards. Is it good form to pin your own stuff to Pinterest? You bet it is.

Pin Your Personal Pictures

First, you can use Pinterest as kind of an online photo scrapbook. Just as you fill your own physical scrapbooks with pictures of your friends and family, so can you fill your Pinterest pinboards.

In fact, using Pinterest to collect and share personal photos makes a lot of sense. You can create individual pinboards for different kinds of photos—vacation pics, holidays, you name it. Then upload photos from your computer as new pins, and you have instant photo albums.

Pinboard for personal photos ———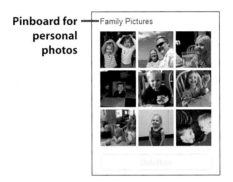

You can target your photo pinboards for your own personal use, or share a pinboard's URL with friends and family so they can view the photos, too. Just go to the pinboard you want to share and copy the web address from the top of your web browser. Paste the URL into an email message and your friends and family need only click the link in the message to view the photos you're sharing.

EVERYONE SEES EVERYTHING

The issue of pinning personal items is potentially harmful as Pinterest does not currently offer any controls over who can and cannot see your pins. That is, there's no way to make a specific pin or board private; everything pinned is public, so everyone can see everything. Think twice, then, before pinning private photos or items to a Pinterest board, as it will be visible to potentially tens of millions of Pinterest users. (And that includes subtly private items, such as a photo of you standing in front of your mailbox, complete with the street address on the side.)

Pin Stuff You Create

Many people are using Pinterest to share and promote items that they create. Artists are pinning paintings and sculptures; designers are pinning rooms they've worked on; photographers are pinning photos they've shot. It's all good, and it's encouraged by the Pinterest community.

You can pin photos of anything to a pinboard. That includes craft and hobby items you've personally created, or more professional items that you have for sale.

Homemade craft

Pinterest is a great place to share your hobbies and interests. There's a definite creative bent to the community, and you're likely to find lots of people interested in the art and crafts you create. It doesn't matter what kind of item you're into—fashion, crafts, photography, you name it—there's probably lots of other people on Pinterest who share your interests. So go ahead and pin photos of what you create; you might be surprised at the audience you attract.

Pin Items You're Selling

Pinterest isn't just for lookers, it's also for buyers and sellers. To that end, if you have art or crafts for sale, Pinterest is a great way to promote the items you create.

As noted, Pinterest is especially friendly to the creative community. It's likely that you'll find lots of potential customers for any items you have for sale. All you have to do is pin a good photograph of the item, give it an appealing description, and pin it to the appropriate pinboard. From there, let Pinterest to its thing and you'll soon find interested users discovering what you've created. Make sure the pin links back to your website, where you can close the deal.

Item for sale —

For that matter, many retailers are using Pinterest to promote items that they sell. For example, if you sell used clothing, you can pin photos of specific garments to your pinboards. Pinterest has a lot of fashion followers, and when they discover your item, they'll click through to your site.

The key is to post items of interest to the Pinterest community, accompanied by the appropriate promotional description. If it's something of interest, Pinterest does the rest.

HASHTAGS AND PRICES

If you want to use Pinterest to sell your goods, you need to make sure that interested customers can find your pins. To that end, you want to include hashtags for the primary keywords that describe your items. Just put the hashtag character (#) in front of those words you think potential customers might be searching for.

In addition, it never hurts to put prices on the items you have for sale. Just enter the dollar symbol ($) before the price, and Pinterest adds a price banner to the pinned image, and include it in the Gifts section of the site. That's free promotion for you!

Don't Just Pin Your Own Stuff

Even if you're using Pinterest to showcase items you've made or have for sale, you don't want to make that the sole focus of your Pinterest activity. Yes, you can use Pinterest for self-promotion, but that shouldn't be your only presence on the site.

If you want to attract the largest number of followers, you need to expand your offerings to include other items of interest to those folks. Yes, they're interested in what you have to offer, but they're also interested in other stuff. It's okay to include photos of similar items in your pinboards, and to post pins that showcase related techniques or ideas.

In other words, mix your own pins with other pins that provide value to your followers. They'll thank you for the information.

What Not to Pin

With all this advice on the many different things you can pin, are there things you should shy away from pinning? You bet there are.

Don't Pin from a Google Image Search

The "Always Pin from the Original Source" section covered the importance of pinning from the original source. Well, one common mistake that some pinners make is pinning directly from an image found in a Google image search. That is, you search Google for an image, then either try to pin the thumbnail image on the search results page or the larger image you get when you click on the thumbnail.

Unfortunately, this creates a pin that links back to Google, not to the website where the image actually resides. Anyone clicking your pin sees the search results or image result page on the Google site—which isn't what you want them to see.

Instead, you need to click through the thumbnail and the image result page to the actual website for that image. Then you can create your pin, which links to the proper page.

Google image search result page—
don't pin from here

Click to view the
hosting website

Links back to Google,
not the hosting website

Cute kitten.

google.com

Don't Change the Link Address

Every pin you create includes a link back to the original web page. The detailed URL is presented when you create the pin; anyone who clicks the pin is taken to this web page.

You can edit the host URL after you've created a pin, however, you should not do this. Some unscrupulous pinners change the URL to link back to their own websites instead of to the site with the original content. Anyone who clicks on an edited link is redirected to a different site, which can benefit the other site at the detriment of the original one.

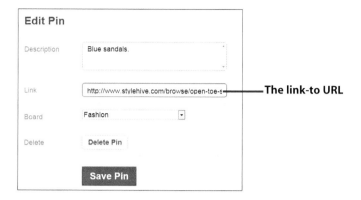

The link-to URL

You don't want to trick your Pinterest followers in this way. Editing a URL to redirect people to your own website is dishonest. Don't do it.

Don't Copy and Paste a Pin's Description

As previously mentioned, every pin should be accompanied by a text description. This description should be yours—that is, your own description of the item, in your own words. It should not be someone else's description that you cut and paste from another site.

Provide an original description

It's tempting to just cut and paste the description of an item from the host site, especially when you're talking about step-by-step instructions and the like. Unfortunately, this is stealing content, not sharing it.

Anyone clicking on the pin will see the host site's content, anyway, so there's little point in duplicating in your pin's description. Take the effort to describe a pin in your own words; your followers will find your own impressions of the item more valuable, in any case.

Repinning

The only exception to reusing someone else's description comes when you repin an item found on the Pinterest site. When repinning, you can keep the original description, or to replace it with one of your own. Either approach is acceptable.

Don't Pin Things That Are Private

This one should go without saying, but I'm going to say it anyway. Pinterest is a public forum; anything you pin is viewable by anyone else on the Web. Don't post items that are meant to be private. Keep private images private—don't make them public on Pinterest.

Don't Pin Inappropriate Images

Along the same lines, know that Pinterest has a terms of service that describes what you can and cannot post. When it comes to pinning what Pinterest calls "objectionable content," if you're caught at it by other users, Pinterest deletes the pins in question.

What's objectionable to Pinterest? Here's the short list:

- Nudity or pornography

- Graphic violence

- Attacks on an individual or group

- Hateful speech or symbols

- Spam

If you happen to see a pin with this kind of objectionable content, click to the detailed pin page and then click the Report Pin button. You can then tell Pinterest what kind of objectionable content you've found and let the site investigate.

In addition, you should not post an item that is someone else's intellectual property. We're talking copyright infringement here, which means you can't claim an image or item as your own if it's not. For example, you can't post a photo taken by someone else and say it's yours. If a copyright owner finds an infringing item, he can report it to Pinterest for investigation and possible deletion.

Reporting objectionable content

REPORTING A COPYRIGHT VIOLATION

If you're a copyright owner who finds a violation on the Pinterest site, you can report the violation to Pinterest. You need to identify and provide the URL of the infringing pin in the form of a Notice of Alleged Infringement, as per the Digital Millennium Copyright Act of 1998. Send the Notice of Alleged Infringement to the following address:

Pinterest Copyright Agent
635 High Street
Palo Alto, CA 94301

You can also email the notice to copyright@pinterest.com, or call Pinterest directly at 650-561-5407. Pinterest will duly investigate your claim and, if it finds in your favor, delete the offending pin.

Pinterest's
iPhone app

→ Logging in from your iPhone

→ Viewing pins on your iPhone

→ Liking, repinning, and commenting on pins

→ Sharing pins via Facebook, Twitter, and email

→ Creating a Pin It bookmarklet

→ Pinning from web pages and your iPhone's camera

Using Pinterest on Your iPhone

You're not limited to pinning and browsing Pinterest on your computer. If you have an iPhone, you can use Pinterest wherever you go and whatever you're doing. All you have to do is install Pinterest's iPhone app; then you can view all your own pins, view pins from people you follow, browse pins by category, and even create new pins right from your iPhone screen.

You can download and install the Pinterest app from Apple's iPhone App Store; it's free. Just search for **pinterest** and follow the instructions from there.

Signing Into Your Pinterest Account

After you've installed the Pinterest iPhone app, you should see a Pinterest icon on your iPhone screen. Tap this icon to launch the Pinterest app.

iPhone Only

As of April 2012, Pinterest does not offer a dedicated iPad app, nor apps for Android or other mobile operating systems. The only mobile app currently offered is for the Apple iPhone—although you can use this app on your iPad. If you have another type of smartphone or tablet, you can still access the Pinterest website from your device's web browser.

Pinterest on Windows 7 Phones

Although Pinterest does not offer an official app for Windows 7 phones, there is a third-party app that offers Pinterest functionality. It's called Pinspiration, and you can find it in Microsoft's Windows Phone Marketplace.

>>>*step-by-step*

Logging In

The first time you launch the Pinterest app, you need to log into your Pinterest account. Pinterest should keep you logged in for subsequent visits.

You Need a Pinterest Account

You must have a Pinterest account to use the Pinterest iPhone app.

1. Tap the Pinterest icon to launch the Pinterest app.

2. Tap the Login with Facebook button to log in using your Facebook ID. This launches the Facebook app; tap the Allow All button.

3. Tap the Login with Twitter button to log in using your Twitter ID. This displays the Connect to Twitter dialog box; enter your Twitter username and password and then tap the Return button.

4. Enter your email address into the Email field and your Pinterest password into the Password box to log in with your email address.

5. Tap the Login button.

Logging Out

Pinterest should keep you logged in for subsequent sessions. You can, however, log out of your Pinterest account at any time.

1. Tap the Profile icon at the bottom of any screen to display your profile page.

2. Tap the Account button.

3. Tap the red Logout button.

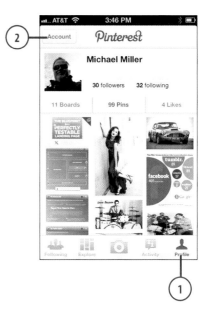

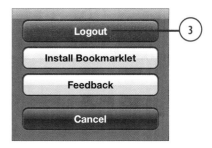

Viewing Pins

The Pinterest app makes it easy to view pins on your iPhone. You can view pins from people you follow, or just browse pins by general category.

>>>step-by-step

Browsing Pins from People You Follow

The Pinterest iPhone app features a navigation bar at the bottom of the screen. Tap the icons on the navigation bar to perform specific activities, such as browsing pins from the people you follow.

1. Tap the Following icon at the bottom of the screen. This displays the most recent pins from the people you follow. Scroll down the screen to view older pins.

2. Tap a pin to view the image on its original web page.

3. Tap the Close button to return to Pinterest.

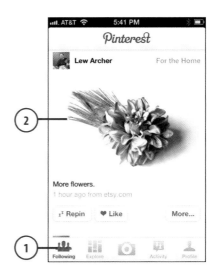

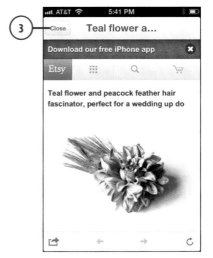

Browsing Pins by Category

You can also browse all pins on the Pinterest site, by category.

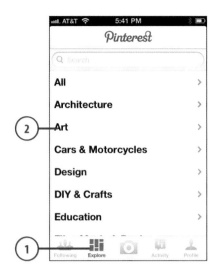

1. Tap the Explore icon at the bottom of the screen. This displays a list of Pinterest categories.

2. Tap a category to display thumbnails of pins within the category.

3. Tap a thumbnail to display the full pinned image and description.

Liking, Repinning, and Commenting on a Pin

The Pinterest app lets you like, repin, comment on, and share pins from your iPhone. You can even save pinned images to your iPhone's camera roll.

>>>step-by-step

Liking a Pin

Liking a pin is as simple as clicking a button.

1. Navigate to the pin you want to like and scroll to the bottom of the pin.

2. Tap the Like button.

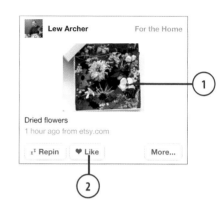

Repinning a Pin

You can easily repin any item you like to your own pinboards.

1. Scroll to the bottom of the pin and tap the Repin button. This displays the Repin screen.

2. Edit the current description at the top of the screen, or enter a new description.

3. Tap Board to display your list of pinboards.

4. Tap the board you want to pin to.

5. To share this pin on Facebook, tap "on" the Facebook switch.

6. To share this pin on Twitter, tap "on" Twitter and, when prompted, enter your Twitter username and password.

7. Tap the Repin button at the top-right corner of the screen.

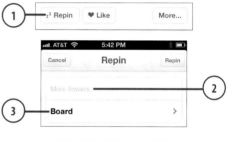

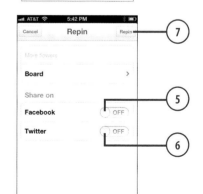

Commenting on a Pin

Assuming you can use the iPhone's onscreen virtual keyboard, it's easy to add a comment to any pin you like.

1. Scroll to the bottom of the pin and tap the More button.

2. Tap the Comment button.

3. Enter your comment into the text box.

4. Tap the blue Send button.

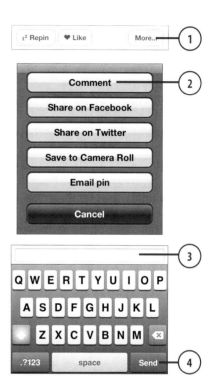

Saving a Pinned Image to Your Camera Roll

You can save any pinned image to your iPhone's camera roll and then view that picture on your iPhone at any time.

1. Scroll to the bottom of the pin and tap the More button.

2. Tap the Save to Camera Roll button.

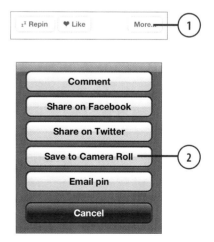

Sharing a Pin

The Pinterest iPhone app lets you share pins you like via Facebook, Twitter, and email.

>>>*step-by-step*

Sharing via Facebook

If you logged into the Pinterest app with your Facebook account, it's easy to post a pin to your Facebook news feed as a status update.

1. Scroll to the bottom of the pin and tap the More button.

2. Tap the Share on Facebook button to display the Share Pin screen.

3. Edit the existing description or enter any additional text into the main text box.

4. Tap the Share button.

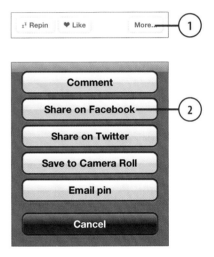

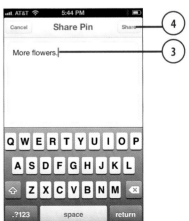

>>>step-by-step

Sharing via Twitter

You can also share a link to any pin as a tweet to your Twitter followers.

1. Scroll to the bottom of the pin and tap the More button.

2. Tap the Share on Twitter button.

Sign In

If prompted, enter your Twitter user-name and password and then tap Return.

3. When the Share Pin screen appears, edit the existing descrip-tion or enter any additional text into the main text box.

4. Tap the Share button.

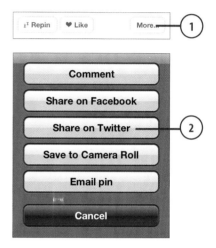

>>>step-by-step

Sharing via Email

If you want to share a pin with someone who is not on one of the major social networks, you can do so via your iPhone's built-in email app.

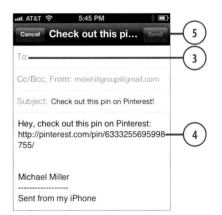

1. Scroll to the bottom of the pin and tap the More button.

2. Tap the Email Pin button to display the email screen.

3. Enter the recipient's address into the To: field.

4. Edit the email message, if you like.

5. Tap the Send button.

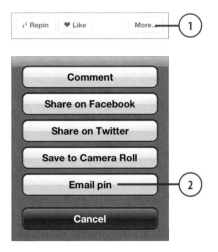

Viewing Your Pins and Activity

The Pinterest iPhone app provides access to everything you've posted to Pinterest. This includes all your pins and pinboards. You can also view any recent activity regarding your pins—who's liked, commented on, or repinned your pins.

>>>step-by-step

Viewing Your Boards and Pins

Your Pinterest profile is fully accessible from your iPhone. Your boards, pins, and likes are displayed on separate tabs on the Profile screen.

1. Tap the Profile button at the bottom of any screen to display your Profile page.

2. Tap the Boards tab to view a list of your pinboards. Tap a pinboard to view the pins on that board.

3. Tap the Pins tab to view your most recent pins. Tap a pin to view it full screen.

4. Tap the Likes tab to view all the pins you've liked. Tap a pin to view it full screen.

5. Tap the Followers tab to view a list of people who are following you.

6. Tap the Following tab to view a list of people you're following.

Viewing Your Recent Activity

You can also view a list of recent activity regarding your account—people you've liked, commented on, and repinned your pins.

1. Tap the Activity icon at the bottom of any screen. This displays your recent activity list.

2. Tap any person's name to view his or her Pinterest profile.

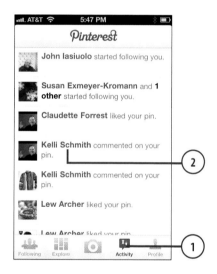

Pinning from Your iPhone

It's easy enough to use your iPhone to find and view pins. But you can also use it to create pins—with a little preparation beforehand.

>>>step-by-step

Installing the Pin It Bookmarklet

Before you can pin from a web page, you first have to install the Pin It bookmarklet in your iPhone's Safari web browser.

1. Tap the Profile icon at the bottom of any screen to display your profile page.

2. Tap the Account button to display the Account menu.

3. Tap the Install Bookmarklet button to open the Safari web browser and go to the bookmarklet installation page.

4. Tap the middle icon at the bottom of the browser.

5. Tap the Add Bookmark button.

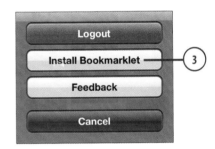

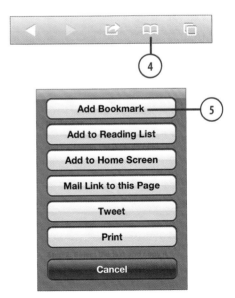

6. Tap the Save button.

7. Back in the Safari browser, tap within the scrolling text in the step 2 section and then tap and hold to display the Select and Select All buttons.

8. Tap Select All.

9. Tap Copy.

10. Tap Done.

11. Tap the Bookmarks button at the bottom of the browser to display the list of bookmarks.

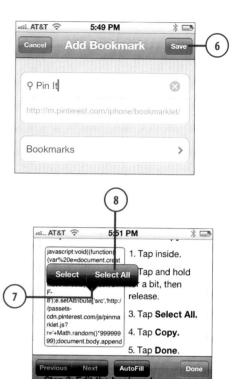

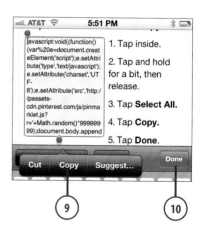

12. Tap the Edit button.

13. Tap the Pin It bookmark.

14. Tap the bookmark's URL to select it.

15. Tap the X next to the URL to clear the field.

16. Tap within the URL field and tap Paste.

17. Tap the Done button.

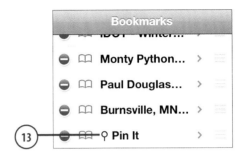

Pinning from a Web Page

After you've created the Pin It book-marklet, it's a relatively simple process to pin an image from any web page you encounter.

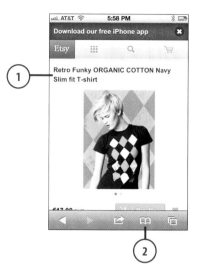

1. Use the Safari browser to navigate to the web page that contains the content you want to pin.

2. Tap the Bookmarks icon at the bottom of the screen to display your list of bookmarks.

3. Tap the Pin It bookmark.

4. You now see a screen of images from this web page. Tap the image you want to pin.

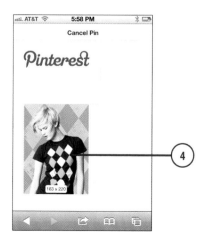

5. This opens the Pinterest app and displays the Add a Pin page. Enter a description of the pin into the top text box.

6. Tap Board to display a list of your pinboards.

7. Tap the board you want to pin to.

8. To share this pin on Facebook, tap "on" the Facebook switch.

9. To share this pin on Twitter, tap "on" Twitter and, when prompted, enter your Twitter username and password.

10. When ready, tap the Pin It button at the top-right corner of the screen.

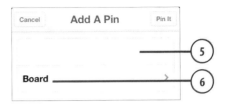

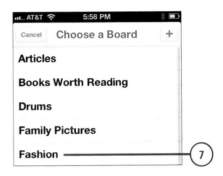

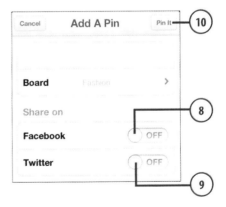

Pinning with the iPhone Camera

There's another way to create pins with your iPhone. You can use your iPhone camera to take a picture of something interesting and then pin that picture to a pinboard.

>>>step-by-step

1. Tap the camera icon at the bottom of any screen in the Pinterest app. This activates your iPhone's camera.

2. Aim your camera at the item you want to pin and then tap the camera icon to shoot the picture.

3. Tap the screen and drag your finger to adjust the photo's lighting.

4. Tap the Use button to return to the Add a Pin page in the Pinterest app.

Use Location

If Pinterest asks to use your current location, tap OK.

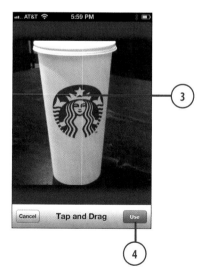

5. Enter a description of your pin into the top text box.

6. Tap Board to display a list of your pinboards.

7. Tap the board you want to pin to.

8. To share this pin on Facebook, tap "on" the Facebook switch.

9. To share this pin on Twitter, tap "on" Twitter and, when prompted, enter your Twitter username and password.

10. When ready, tap the Pin It button at the top-right corner of the screen.

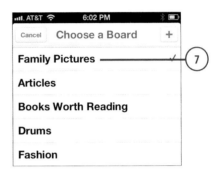

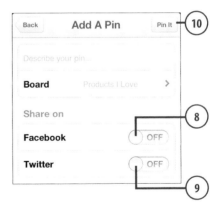

Pinning an Existing Photo from Your iPhone

You can also pin any photo you've taken with your iPhone. It's a matter of uploading the photo from your iPhone's camera roll.

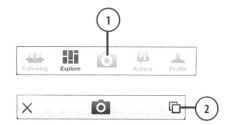

1. Tap the camera icon at the
   bottom of any screen in the
   Pinterest app.

2. Tap the files icon at the lower-
   right side of the screen. This displays a list of all the Photos fold-
   ers on your iPhone.

3. Tap any folder to open it.

4. Tap the photo you want to pin.

5. Use your fingers to move or scale
   the photo, if you wish.

6. Tap the blue Choose button.

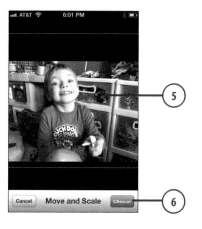

7. Tap the screen and drag your finger to adjust the photo's lighting.

8. Tap the Use button to return to the Add a Pin page in the Pinterest app.

9. Enter a description of your pin into the top text box.

10. Tap Board to display a list of your pinboards.

11. Tap the board you wish to pin to.

12. To share this pin on Facebook, tap "on" the Facebook switch.

13. To share this pin on Twitter, tap "on" Twitter and, when prompted, enter your Twitter username and password.

14. When ready, tap the Pin It button at the top-right corner of the screen.

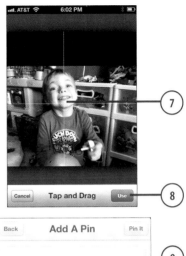

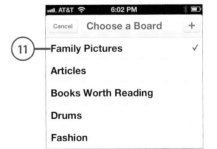

Pin It button in a
blog post

Pin it

Check out this cool new thermostat:

In this chapter, you learn how to add Pin It buttons to your website or blog, so your visitors can pin content from your site.

→ Adding a Pin It button to a blog or web page
→ Adding a Pinterest Follow button to a blog or web page
→ Embedding a pin in a blog post or web page
→ Keeping content on your site from being pinned

Adding Pin It Buttons to Your Website or Blog

If you have your own personal website or blog, you might have content that others would like to pin to Pinterest. In most cases, it's in your own best interest to have your content pinned; it ultimately drives more visitors to your site.

Although anyone can pin any image from your website by using the Pin It button installed in their web browsers, you can make it even easier to pin content by adding a Pin It button to your blog or web page. Visitors can then pin your site content by clicking the Pin It button on your website.

You can also add a Pinterest Follow button to your site; visitors click this button to follow you on Pinterest. Pinterest also lets you embed individual pins in your blog or web pages, which is great for highlighting interesting items, especially in blog posts. And if you'd rather people *not* pin content from your site, you can do that, too—all it takes is a simple line of code.

Adding a Pin It Button to a Blog or Web Page

You can add a Pin It button to any page on your website, to your main blog page, or to any individual blog post. Where you add each button depends on your own personal site strategy.

A Pin It button on a web page

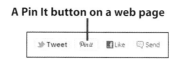

If you have pinnable content on your website, you should add a Pin It button to each applicable web page. Anyone clicking this button then has the option of pinning any image on this page, which then links back to the page itself.

If you have your own blog, you can opt to install the Pin It button on the main blog page or in individual blog posts. A Pin It button on your main blog page links back to that page, not to any individual post. A Pin It button within an individual post links back to that post via the post's unique permalink.

Linking to Blog Posts

For most bloggers, you probably want to add Pin It buttons to individual posts. In general, it's the content of a specific post that people want to pin, not the entire content of your blog. Add the button code to the HTML for each post then visitors can pin each post's content individually.

Adding a Pin It button to a blog or web page requires you to generate a short piece of HTML code to create the button. You then insert that code into the underlying code for your blog or web page, and the button appears when the page is saved and refreshed.

Social Buttons

Chances are you already have buttons on your website for Facebook, Twitter, and other social networks. Pinterest recommends putting the Pin It button adjacent to these other social buttons to increase the social awareness of your content.

>>>step-by-step

1. Click About in the Pinterest navigation bar.

2. Click Pin It Button from the drop-down menu to display Pinterest's main Help page.

3. Make sure the Goodies tab is selected in the left sidebar, to display the Goodies page.

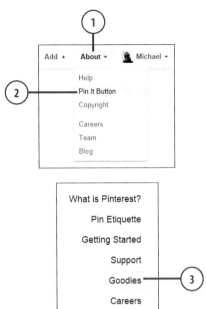

Goodies Page

You can go directly to the Pinterest Goodies page at www.pinterest.com/about/goodies.

4. Scroll to the "Pin It" Button for Websites section and enter the URL of the page where you want the button to appear into the first URL box.

5. Enter the full URL, including filename, of the image to be pinned into the second URL box.

6. Enter an optional description of the pin into the Description box.

7. Pull down the Pin Count list and select how you want the Pin It button and pin count to be displayed—horizontal, vertical, or with no pin count.

8. Make sure the Basic option is selected.

9. Highlight the code in the box at the bottom of this section and then press Ctrl+Ins (Mac: Command+C) to copy this code.

Use the HTML editing program of your choice to open the underlying code of the web page or blog where you want the button to appear, and paste the copied code into your page's code. When you save and update your web page, the Pin It button is available for site visitors.

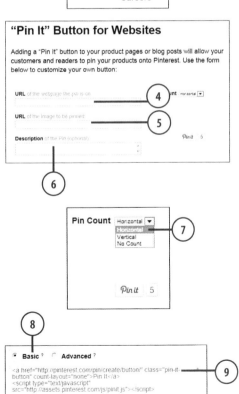

MULTIPLE BUTTONS

Use the Basic option to place a single Pin It button on a web page. To place multiple buttons on a single page, select the Advanced option. This generates code that links to a particular section of the web page. Make sure to insert the Advanced code next to the associated image on the web page.

It's Not All Good

KNOW YOUR CODE

You should only attempt to embed a button or pin on your website if you're familiar and comfortable with HTML and website design. If you're not, find someone slightly more technical to do this for you.

Adding a Follow Button to Your Website or Blog

If you want your website or blog visitors to follow you on Pinterest, you can make it easy for them by adding a Pinterest Follow button to your blog or web page. Anyone clicking this button is taken to Pinterest and prompted to follow your account.

>>>*step-by-step*

1. Click About in the Pinterest navigation bar.

2. Click Help from the drop-down menu to display Pinterest's main Help page.

3. Click the Goodies tab in the left sidebar to display the Goodies page and scroll to the "Follow Button" for Websites section.

Goodies Page

You can go directly to the Pinterest Goodies page at www.pinterest.com/about/goodies.

---

4. Click the type of button you want to use. There are four styles available.

5. Highlight the code in the box next to the button you selected and then press Ctrl+Ins (Mac: Command+C) to copy this code.

Use the HTML editing program of your choice to open the underlying code of the web page or blog where you want the button to appear, and paste the copied code into your page's code. When you save and update your web page, the Follow button is available for site visitors.

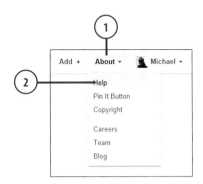

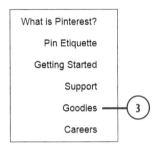

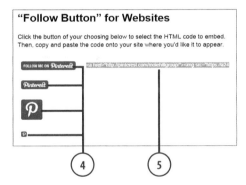

Embedding a Pin on Your Blog or Web Page

If you're a Pinterest user with your own website, you might want to display some of your favorite pins on a page on your site. Likewise, many bloggers like to effectively merge their blogs with their Pinterest accounts by blogging about their favorite pins.

>>>step-by-step

Pinterest enables you to share pinned items by embedding a link to a pin in the code for your web page or blog. To generate the code for embedding a pin, follow these steps:

1. From within Pinterest, navigate to the pin you want to display on your blog or web page and click it to display the detailed pin panel.

2. Click the Embed button to the right of the image to display the Embed Pin on Your Blog panel.

3. Accept the image width and height dimensions or enter different dimensions based on your particular blog or web page.

4. Highlight the code in the box at the bottom of this panel and then press Ctrl+Ins to copy this code.

Paste the copied code into the underlying code on your blog or web page. When you save and upload the blog post or web page that contains the Pinterest embed code, the pin you selected is displayed. Visitors who click on the embedded image are taken to the pin on the Pinterest site.

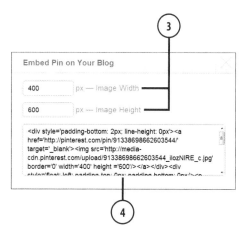

Blue sandals.

stylehive.com

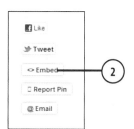

Like

Tweet

Embed

Report Pin

Email

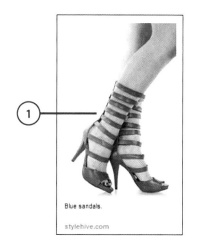

Embed Pin on Your Blog

400   px — Image Width

600   px — Image Height

```
<div style='padding-bottom: 2px; line-height: 0px'><a
href='http://pinterest.com/pin/91338698662603544/'
target='_blank'><img src='http://media-
cdn.pinterest.com/upload/91338698662603544_ilozNIRE_c.jpg'
border='0' width='400' height ='600'/></a></div><div
style='float: left: padding top: 0px: padding bottom: 0px
```

Keeping People from Pinning Your Website Content

Not everyone wants their website or blog content to be pinned. Perhaps you have copyrighted content that you don't want disseminated around the Web; maybe you just don't like the idea of Pinterest users indiscriminately pinning your personal content.

Whatever the case, Pinterest offers a small piece of "no pin" code that keeps web page content from being pinned to the Pinterest site. When this code is inserted on a web page, anyone trying to pin that page sees the following message:

"This site doesn't allow pinning to Pinterest. Please contact the owner with any questions. Thanks for visiting!"

>>>*step-by-step*

1. Use your HTML editing program to open the home page of your website and navigate to the <HEAD> section.

2. Add the following line to the <HEAD> section of the web page:

```
<meta name="pinterest" content="nopin" />
```

When you save and upload the web page, pinning from your entire website is prohibited.

```
<head>
<!-- #BeginEditable "doctitle" -->
<title>Michael Miller: The Molehill Group</title>
<meta name="pinterest" content="nopin" />
```

Add It Once
You need only add the "no pin" code to a single page on your site. After you've added the code, pinning is prohibited from all pages on your site. To restore pinning privileges, simply remove the "no pin" code.

Michael Miller

Michael Miller is a popular writer, with more than 100 how-to books published in the past two decades. Look for his upcoming book, MY PINTEREST, at a bookstore near you.

 Twin Cities, MN

In this chapter, you learn how to use
Pinterest for self-promotion, and how to
gain more Pinterest followers.

→ Learn how to use Pinterest for self-promotion
→ Discover how to promote your Pinterest activity
→ Find out how to increase your number of followers

Promoting Yourself on Pinterest

Pinterest supposedly isn't about self-promotion, but that doesn't mean you can't use Pinterest to promote yourself online. The more people who follow you and view your pins, the more effective you're using Pinterest to promote yourself.

Of course, to be effective in using Pinterest for self-promotion, you have to attract followers to your pins and pinboards. There are many things you can do to draw attention to your Pinterest activity—including integrating Pinterest with other social networks.

Using Pinterest for Self-Promotion

Pinterest is a great venue for promoting yourself. Whether you're an individual who wants to make a bigger name for yourself or a professional who wants to gain more clients for your services, Pinterest can be a key part of your (self) promotional efforts.

When you employ Pinterest for your own personal use, you provide your followers with useful insight into your personality. The kinds of things you pin can tell others a lot about you—what you like, what you find interesting, even your own personal style. It's all a matter of being conscious of everything you do on the Pinterest site—from creating your profile to organizing your pinboards.

Pump Up Your Pinterest Profile

Your self-promotion on Pinterest starts with your profile. You need more than just a bare-bones profile; for people to really get to know you, you have to take advantage of every possible input available.

First, and most obvious, you need to enter your first and last name, the way that you want to be known or think that others might know you as. You should also devise a username that is similar. Don't go for obscure nicknames or references; try to incorporate your real name into your username. For example, if you're Tom Smith (and assuming the username **tomsmith** is already taken, which it is), try a variation such as **tomsmith2012** or **tomsmithchicago** or something similar.

Next, and vitally important, you need to enter a good biography into your profile's About field. Don't leave it blank, and don't slide by with a brief sentence or two. Use the About field to tell others about yourself—who you are, what you do, what you like, and so forth. Don't be shy; put in as much information as can fit in a single paragraph.

Your Description

Your description of yourself appears on your personal Pinterest page, directly below your profile picture.

Pumping up your profile also includes adding an attractive profile picture of yourself. If you're promoting a professional image, make sure it's a profession-al photo; if you're more casual then go with something a little looser. Make sure your photo reflects your personality that you're trying to promote.

Adding a Profile Picture

Learn more about adding a profile picture (and editing the rest of your profile, too) in Chapter 22, "Managing Your Pinterest Account."

Include Links to Your Website, Blog, and Social Network Profiles

Beneath your personal profile are three possible buttons (plus a fourth loca-tion button if you've entered your location). The first can link to your personal blog or website; the second to your Twitter profile page; and the third to your Facebook timeline page.

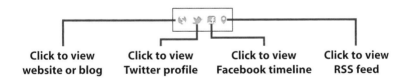

| **Click to view website or blog** | **Click to view Twitter profile** | **Click to view Facebook timeline** | **Click to view RSS feed** |

RSS Feed

People can subscribe to your Pinterest RSS feed to be notified of and view all new pins you make, via a newsreader program.

You want to display all these buttons, as they enable your followers to click to learn more about you on other sites. This means doing the following from your Edit Profile page:

- Enter your blog or website URL into the Website box

- Switching "on" the Link to Facebook switch

- Switching "on" the Link to Twitter switch

Editing Your Profile

Learn how to edit your Pinterest profile in Chapter 22, "Managing Your Pinterest Account," and how to connect Pinterest to other social networks in Chapter 11, "Sharing Pins to Facebook and Twitter."

Pin Steadily

If you want people to follow you, you have to give them a lot of things to follow. That means pinning frequently and steadily. One pin a week won't do it; you need to pin daily in order to keep your followers' attention.

You also don't want to bombard your followers with huge numbers of pins all at once. Don't go for a week without pinning and then pin a dozen items one right after another. Try to space out your pins to maximize your exposure—and engagement with your followers.

Pin from Many Sources

Your pinning gets boring if all your pins come from a handful of sources. You need to pin from a variety of different sites, not just one or two, to keep it interesting for your followers.

Think of Your Followers

Speaking of your followers, if you want to promote yourself, you have to think not of what you like, but what your followers like to see. That is, to get people to know and like you on Pinterest, you need to pin items that others find interesting and useful.

Self-promotion is not solely a matter of talking about yourself; it's also about talking about what value you bring to others. To that end, you need to think about what your followers want to see, and then give that to them—in the form of pins. Pin items that your followers find interesting, and they'll follow you more closely, and recommend you to their friends.

Let Your Pins Reflect Your Personality

Of course, Pinterest self-promotion isn't all about pinning for your followers. Your pins are the way your followers get to know you, and as such should reflect your personality and interests. Think of your followers, yes, but don't do so at the expense of yourself. Pin items that represent who you really are, not some fictional person you will never be.

Look for "Pinnable" Images

Given that Pinterest is a visual medium, you need to think visually. With every Pinterest page displaying dozens if not hundreds of images, you need to make sure your pins stand out from the rest, visually.

That means looking for "pinnable" images that others will find appealing and worth clicking. It's a fact of life; visually appealing images are more likely to get clicked and repinned than less appealing images.

What makes a "pinnable" image? Think bold and simple, something that stands out from the visual clutter that is Pinterest. High-contrast images work best—something bright against a plain white background, for example. Let your own instincts be your guide; if an image stands out for you, it probably will for your followers, as well.

A "pinnable" image—bold and simple

A less appealing image

More flowers

Dried flowers

etsy.com

etsy.com

It's Not All Good

KEEP IT SHORTER

When it comes to picking images to pin, think of how they fit on the Pinterest page. Really long images (such as what you find in some infographics) take up too much space and might even require scrolling to see the whole thing. Avoid longer images and instead pick shorter images, closer to square, that fit better on the page.

Pin Videos

If you want to stand out from the Pinterest crowd, post some videos. The vast majority of pins are of images; few pinners, at this stage of the game, are pinning videos. Search YouTube for videos your followers might find interesting and then pin them. The sheer uniqueness of a video pin attracts a lot of eyeballs on the Pinterest site.

A video pin —

Holiday Braided Updo

7 likes 28 repins

Natalia F onto Hair & Make-up

Pinning Videos

Learn more about pinning YouTube videos in Chapter 7, "Pinning and Playing Videos."

Pin on the Go

Don't limit your pins to items you find on familiar websites. Get the Pinterest iPhone app and start pinning on the go. You can use the iPhone app to take pictures when you're out, and then upload those pictures as pins. You can even add location information to your mobile pins so that anyone searching by location will find them. It's a great way to expand your pinning repertoire.

Pinterest iPhone app

Mobile Pinning

Learn more about pinning with the Pinterest iPhone app in Chapter 13, "Using Pinterest on Your iPhone."

Pin Personal Pictures

If you really want to personalize your Pinterest presence, upload some pictures of yourself as pins. A few personal photos pinned to one of your pinboards helps people get to know you and literally puts a personal face on your pins.

A personal photo, pinned

Mike and Sherry

mikeandsherrypictures.blo
gspot.com

Keep It Professional

You don't want to get *too* personal with your pins, especially if you're present-
ing a professional front. Choose photos and other items that reflect your personality, but in a public way.

Pin from Your Blog or Website

When it comes to promoting yourself or the goods and services you offer,
nothing beats pinning items originally posted to your personal blog or website. Every pin you post from your site promotes your site—and even more so
when someone clicks the pin and is taken to your site.

To that end, you should pin each blog post you make, perhaps to a dedicated
"blog posts" pinboard. You should also selectively pin related items from your
website so that your followers know what it is that you do. Just don't over-pin
items from your own blog or site; fit them into the flow of your other pins
from the Web.

Describe Your Pins

Every pin you post should be accompanied by a description. Use words to
describe the images you pin, and to add a personal touch to each item. If
appropriate, you can even including your business name or website URL in
the description.

Remember, the text you write can have a big effect. Because most people
who repin keep the original description, that text should have very long
legs—that is, the text will be repeated over and over and over again.

Pin description

Create Different Boards for Different Activities

Use your pinboards to present different faces or activities to your followers. For example, if you're a craftsperson, you might want to create one pinboard for personal photos and another for the crafts you create. Make it easy for people to find the types of pins they're looking for.

Devise Interesting Names for Your Boards

If you really want to let your personality show, don't go with the default Pinterest boards. Create your own boards and use some imagination when naming them. Interesting and creative board names reflect your personality— and can go a long way in attracting more followers.

For example, instead of naming a board **Recipes**, you might name it **Are You Hungry?** Or instead of Pinterest's default **For the Home** board, name it **My Dream Home**. Or, for a crafts board, something like **Crafty Lady** or **Get Crafty**. You get the idea; a little creativity helps your boards stand out from all the others.

SHAMELESS SELF-PROMOTION

Although you can use Pinterest for self-promotion, you shouldn't be blatant about it. That typically means blending self-promotional pins with more traditional pins of items you find on the Web. It also means avoiding over-pinning items from your own blog or website.

Your pinboards need to tell people about you without sounding like you're bragging. You need to use third-party images to tell your story, along with your own images; keeping the proper mix is essential.

You should also avoid overly promoting yourself when you comment on others' pins. It's tempting to include a link to your blog or website in every comment, but it's not necessary and could be counterproductive.

So shoot for a mix of pins, and try to be modest about things. On Pinterest, a little self-promotion goes a long way.

Promoting Your Pinterest Presence

If you want to maximize the number of followers you have, you need to promote your Pinterest activity. You can do this within the Pinterest community or elsewhere on the Web.

Participate in the Pinterest Community

The quickest and easiest way to gain more followers is to make your presence known to them on Pinterest. That means actively participating in the Pinterest community.

Participating in Pinterest involves more than just pinning to your own pinboards. You need to get out there and discover what others are pinning, and then engage those pinners, socially.

There are a number of ways to engage other users on the Pinterest site, including the following:

- Click the Like button for pins that you truly like

- Comment on pins you find interesting

- Tag other Pinterest users in your pin descriptions (by using the @ character in front of their usernames)

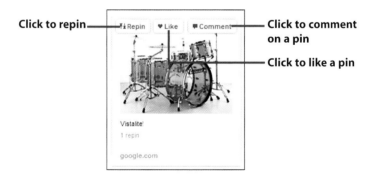

Click to repin ——— Click to comment on a pin

Click to like a pin

Liking and More

Learn more about going further with pins in Chapter 9, "Liking, Repinning, and Commenting."

Repin

Another way to participate socially is to repin items that match your own interests. When you repin an item, the person who pinned that item gets notified via email if she that has that notification option set up. (They also get a credit on your pin.) This helps the other pinner get familiar with you, which can prove beneficial for increasing your number of followers.

Original pinner

New pinner

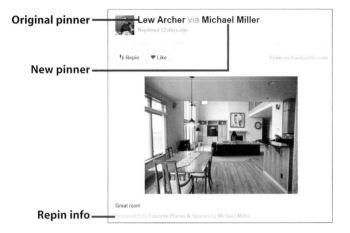

Repin info

Use Hashtags and Keywords

You can help others find the items you pin by including important keywords in the pin's description. Think of how others might search for a particular item and make sure you include those words.

For example, if you collect Precious Moments figurines, you'll want to include the phrase "Precious Moments" somewhere in your pin's description, as well as the word "figurine," and maybe even the word "collectible." These are all ways that others might search for the item you pinned.

In addition, make good use of hashtags in your pin descriptions. Hashtags function as keywords and also let your followers find additional pins for that word or phrase by just clicking on the hashtag.

Integrate Pinterest into Your Other Social Media

Pinterest's connection to other social networks is two-way. Not only can your Pinterest users click to view your Facebook and Twitter accounts, but your Facebook friends and Twitter followers can view the items you pin on Pinterest.

A pin displayed as a Facebook status update

This is a great way to draw more attention to your Pinterest activity. When you post a pin to Facebook as a status update, anyone viewing your news feed sees the pin and, if they like, can click to view it on Pinterest. Same thing when you tweet a pin; Twitter followers can click the link in the tweet to view the pin on the Pinterest site.

A pin linked in a tweet

When you link all your social networking accounts, you essentially broadcast all your pins to Facebook and Twitter with a single effort. It's efficient and it helps promote your Pinterest activity.

Integrate Pinterest into Your Blog or Website

Similarly, you can send people to your Pinterest account from your personal blog or website. In fact, there are two ways to do so:

- Add a Pinterest Follow button to your blog or website. This makes it easy for site visitors to view your Pinterest profile and follow you on Pinterest, if they like.

 **Pinterest Follow button**

- Add a Pin It button to appropriate content on your blog or website. This makes it easy for Pinterest users visiting your site to pin your content.

Pin it—— **Pin It button**

Incorporate both Follow and Pin It buttons to maximize your exposure.

Adding Buttons

Learn how to add Pinterest buttons in Chapter 14, "Adding Pin It Buttons to Your Website or Blog."

SEE WHO'S PINNING FROM YOUR WEBSITE

If you want to view items that have been pinned from your blog or website, and who did the pinning, all you have to do is go to **www.pinterest.com/source/*yoursitehere*/**. For example, to view pins from my website, go to **www.pinterest.com/source/molehilllgroup.com/**. This displays a page of recent pins made from items on the site.

Make Your Activity Visible to Search Engines

You'd be surprised how much traffic you can attract to your Pinterest account from Google and other search engines. Assuming that you create an effective Pinterest profile, and that you pin a variety of interesting items, people searching for specific topics or items see your Pinterest activity in their web search results.

To make your Pinterest activity searchable by Google, Yahoo!, Bing, and other search engines, you have to switch "on" search visibility, which you do from your Edit Profile page. See Chapter 22 for detailed instructions.

**Switch "on" to enable
search visibility**

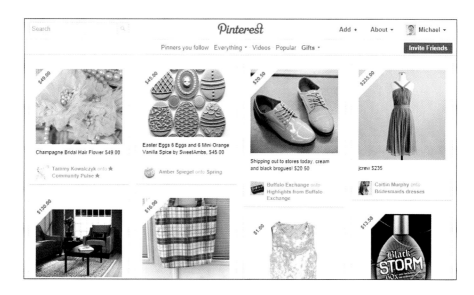

In this chapter, you learn how to find gift ideas on Pinterest.

→ Browsing for gifts
→ Selling gift items on Pinterest

Finding Gifts on Pinterest

One of the things that Pinterest has evolved into is a great gift guide. Many of the items people pin to the site are things they'd like to have given to them, they'd like to give, or they have for sale as gifts. As such, it's fun to browse through Pinterest's Gifts section, looking for items you yourself might like to give or receive.

If you create or sell items that might make good gifts, you can also use Pinterest to promote the items you have for sale. Add a price to your item's description, and it gets listed in Pinterest's Gifts section where other users can click through to purchase the item on your own website.

Browsing for Gifts

Pinterest has a section just for gifts. It's accessible from the home page, by clicking the Gifts link on the filter bar. Items in the Gifts section are uniquely suited for gift giving.

All items in the Gifts section have prices listed in the description and also bannered across the top-left corner of each image. When you click a gift pin, you're typically taken to the site where you can find the item for sale—and, if you like, where you can purchase it.

You can browse all the items in the Gifts section or browse gift items by price. Gifts are organized by the following price ranges:

- $1–$20
- $50–$100
- $200–$500
- $20–$50
- $100–$200
- $500+

>>>step-by-step

1. Click the Pinterest logo at the top of any page to go to Pinterest's home page.

2. Click Gifts in the filter bar to display all gift items.

3. Mouse over Gifts in the filter bar and click the desired price range to filter gifts by a specific price range.

4. All gift items have the selling price displayed in a banner in the top-left corner of the pin. Click the pinned image to display the detailed pin page.

5. Click the pinned image to view the item on its host website—and make a purchase, if you like.

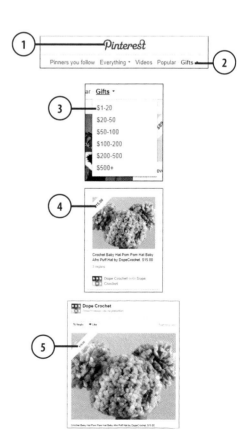

View the Source

All detailed pin pages display the site where the pinned item was originally displayed. If you want to purchase an item, look for host sites that are known online retailers or marketplaces.

ETSY

Many of the items found in Pinterest's Gifts section are found on Etsy (www.etsy.com), an online marketplace for handmade items. Craftspeople of all types post their items on the Etsy site, which then serves as the middleman when customers decide to purchase.

As you can see in the following figure, Etsy uses a similar visual layout as Pinterest. It's only natural for artisans who sell on Etsy to cross-post their items to Pinterest. In addition, many consumers find items they like on Etsy and post them to Pinterest. It's a nice symbiotic relationship.

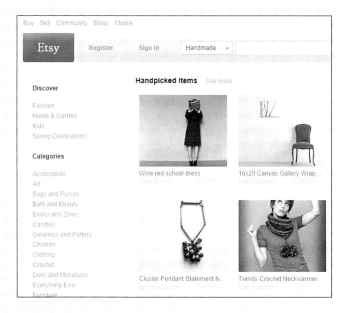

Don't be surprised, then, when you click on a gift item you like on Pinterest to be transported to the Etsy site. In fact, Etsy has its own presence on Pinterest; just go to www.pinterest.com/etsy/ to view all of Etsy's pins.

Pinning Gift Items

Pinterest's Gifts section is also a great way to direct people to items you'd like to receive as a gift. Just make sure to include the gift's price (preceded by a dollar sign or Euro mark) in the pin's description, and it is fed to the Gifts section.

Similarly, Pinterest's Gifts section is a great place to showcase craft items you might have for sale. Again, all you have to do is include the item's price in its description, and it shows up in the Gifts section, complete with price banner.

Price Ranges

Keep Pinterest's default price ranges in mind when you set the price for an item. It's probably better to price an item at $19.99 to hit the $1–$20 range than at $21.00, which moves you up to the $20–$50 range.

>>>step-by-step

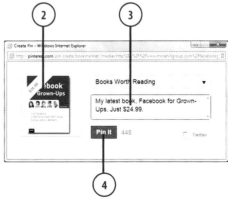

1. Assuming the item you want to showcase or sell is displayed on your website or in an online marketplace, such as Etsy, navigate to the item's web page and click your browser's Pin It button.

2. The Create Pin dialog box displays the image you selected. Create the pin as you would normally.

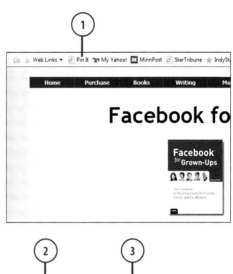

3. In the Describe Your Pin section, make sure you include the item's selling price, preceded by the dollar sign ($).

4. Click the red Pin It button when done.

The item is fed into Pinterest's Gifts section with the price displayed in a banner. Anyone clicking the pin will be taken to your website, where they can learn more about and hopefully purchase the item in question.

Price Banner

The price banner displays anywhere the pin is viewed, not just in the Gifts section. All pins with prices in the description display a price banner.

WHAT SELLS BEST ON PINTEREST?

When it comes to selling items on Pinterest, certain categories sell better than others. Keeping in mind the site's female-skewing demographic, it's not surprising that handcrafted items, artwork, clothing, fashion accessories, jewelry, and the like sell best.

This plays into Pinterest's growing reputation among the arts and crafts community. If you make your own jewelry, artwork, clothing, and the like, Pinterest provides the perfect platform for showcasing your wares. Just make sure you include a useful description along with the item price when you pin; Pinterest and its users will do the rest.

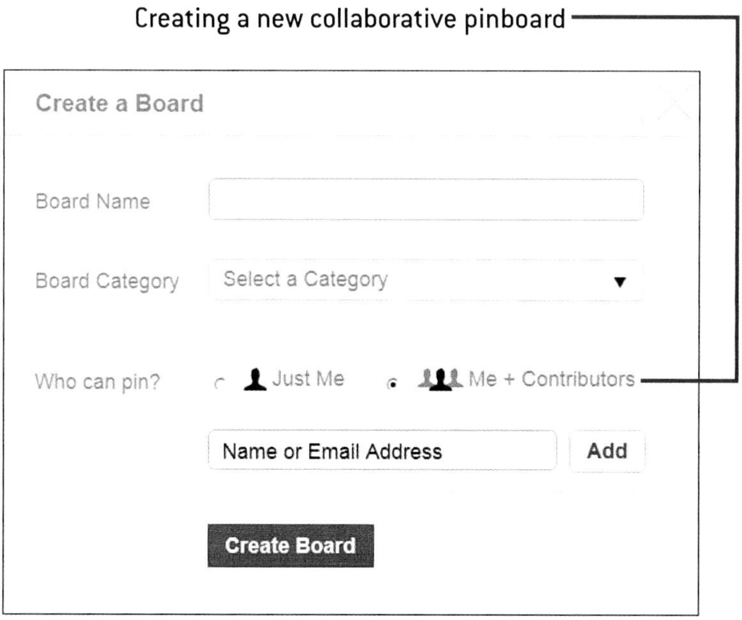

Creating a new collaborative pinboard

Create a Board

Board Name

Board Category   Select a Category   ▼

Who can pin?   ○ 👤 Just Me   ⦿ 👥👥 Me + Contributors

                    Name or Email Address   Add

                    Create Board

In this chapter, you learn how to share information and collaborate on group projects via Pinterest pinboards.

→ Creating and managing collaborative pinboards
→ Sharing group information
→ Collaborating on Pinterest

Using Pinterest for Sharing and Collaboration

Pinterest lets you take virtually any page on the Web and turn it into a pin that can be shared with other Pinterest users. As such, Pinterest can easily function as a vehicle for sharing images, articles, and other content with your friends, family, business associates, and other members of your community.

You can also create so-called collaborative pinboards, where other users can pin to the boards you create. This makes it easier to share information among members of a group, and for members to collaborate on group projects. It doesn't matter whether you're a member of a community organization, a teacher or student in a classroom, or a worker in a large corporation; Pinterest lets you work closer together than you can otherwise.

Managing Collaborative Pinboards

Information sharing and group collaboration is facilitated by Pinterest's collaborative pinboards. Whereas other users can see any information you post to a normal pinboard, making that pinboard collaborative enables selected users post to the board, as well.

>>>step-by-step

Creating a Collaborative Board

By default, each new pinboard you create is a personal board. That is, you are the only person who can pin items to the board. (Others can view the board, of course.)

Pinterest also enables you to create collaborative boards on which other users you specify can also pin items of interest. You configure a board's collaborative status when you first create the board.

1. Click Add+ on the Pinterest menu bar to display the Add panel.

2. Click Create a Board to display the Create a Board panel.

3. Enter the name for the new board into the Board Name box.

4. Pull down the Board Category list and select a category for this board.

5. Go to the Who Can Pin? section and select the Me+Contributors option to expand the panel.

6. Enter a collaborator's Pinterest username or email address into the Name or Email Address box. Pinterest displays a list of potential matches; select the person you want from this list.

7. Click the Add button.

8. Repeat steps 6 and 7 to add additional contributors.

9. Click the red Create Board button.

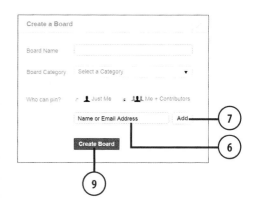

Follow Your Collaborators

To add a person as a contributor to one of your boards, you must first follow that person, or one of her boards.

>>>step-by-step

Making an Existing Board Collaborative

You can also make an existing personal pinboard a collaborative board and then add new collaborators to that board.

1. Mouse over your name in the top-right corner of any Pinterest page.

2. Click Boards from the drop-down menu to display your list of pin-boards.

3. Find the pinboard you want to make collaborative and click that board's Edit button.

4. Scroll down the Edit Board page to the Who Can Pin? section and then click the Me+Contributors option to expand the panel.

5. Enter a collaborator's Pinterest username or email address into the Name or Email Address box. Pinterest now displays a list of potential matches; select the person you want from this list.

6. Click the Add button.

7. Repeat steps 5 and 6 to add additional contributors.

8. Click the red Save Settings button when done.

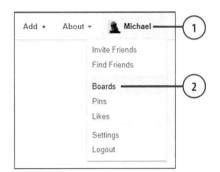

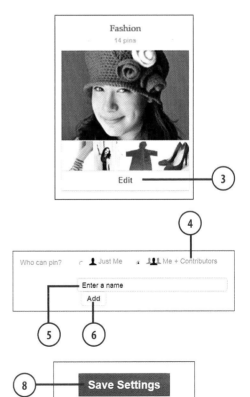

>>>step-by-step

Adding Collaborators to a Board

You can also, at any time, add new collaborators to an existing collaborative board.

1. Mouse over your name in the top-right corner of any Pinterest page.

2. Click Boards from the drop-down menu to display your list of pinboards.

3. Find the collaborative pinboard you want to add people to and click that board's Edit button.

4. Scroll down the Edit Board page to the Who Can Pin? section and then enter the new collaborator's Pinterest username or email address into the Name or Email Address box. Pinterest displays a list of potential matches; select the person you want from this list.

5. Click the Add button.

6. Repeat steps 4 and 5 to add additional contributors.

7. Click the red Save Settings button when done.

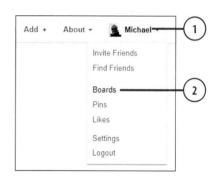

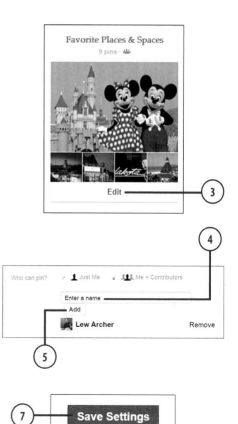

>>>*step-by-step*

Deleting Collaborators from a Board

Over time you might find that one or more collaborators to a board are not pulling their weight and should be removed from the project. For that matter, collaborators might move, change assignments, or otherwise cause themselves to no longer be involved with a project. Fortunately, Pinterest makes it easy to delete collaborators from any group project you've set up.

1. Mouse over your name in the top-right corner of any Pinterest page.

2. Click Boards from the drop-down menu to display your list of pinboards.

3. Find the collaborative pinboard you want to remove people from and then click that board's Edit button.

4. Scroll down the Edit Board page to the Who Can Pin? section, find the person you want to remove from the board, and click Remove next to that person's name.

5. Click the red Save Settings button when done.

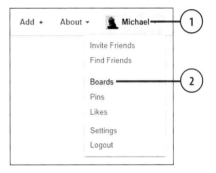

>>>step-by-step

Taking a Collaborative Board Private

You can also, at any time, change a board's status from collaborative to personal. At that point, previous collaborators can still view the board but can no longer contribute to it.

1. Mouse over your name in the top-right corner of any Pinterest page.

2. Click Boards from the drop-down menu to display your list of pinboards.

3. Find the collaborative pinboard you want to make private and then click that board's Edit button.

4. Scroll down the Edit Board page to the Who Can Pin? section and check the Just Me option.

5. Click the red Save Settings button when done.

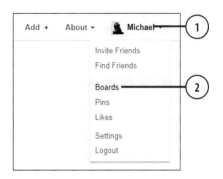

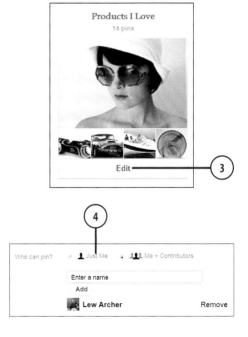

Sharing Group Information on Pinterest

You don't have to make a pinboard collaborative to share information with a group, although you do to share information from a group. To that end, if you're interested in sharing information among a group of co-workers, students, or the like, it's best to create a collaborative board just for that purpose.

There are many different circumstances where you can use Pinterest to share group information. The following sections describe a few.

Sharing Research

One of the more popular uses of Pinterest is as a receptacle for group research. This is typically research for a business or classroom project, but it can also represent research by public or corporate librarians, research assistants, and the like.

For example, you can use Pinterest to keep track of various infographics that might be useful in future projects or research or that you simply find interesting (or think might be interesting to your colleagues). When you find a news article, blog, or website that contains an interesting visual factoid, pin it to a collaborative pinboard created just for that purpose. In this situation, the pinboard functions like a group bookmarking or database system.

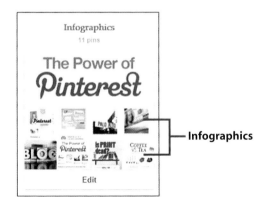

Pinterest is also good for sharing research on community projects. If you serve on a community board or in a community group, you and other group members might run across websites and news stories that are relevant to your community participation. Create a collaborative group for the community group and then encourage all group members to pin interesting and relevant items to the board. All group members, as well as other members of the community, can access the pinned information.

You can also use Pinterest to research projects for your home. When you and your spouse find interesting articles and websites related to a given DIY or rennovation project, pin those items to a collaborative pinboard you've created for that purpose. When it comes time to start work on the project, you have all your research in one place.

— **DYI projects**

Sharing Business Information

The idea of using Pinterest as a visual research database has particular import in a business environment.

Take, for example, the typical business project, where two or more people, typically from different departments (or even different locations) are chosen to work together on a presentation or deliverable of some sort. Group members can pin relevant research to a collaborative Pinterest board and can even use the board to pass around ideas for the project. Because all collaborators can now see what everyone else is thinking and working on, there will be less duplication of effort and a more efficient collaborative process.

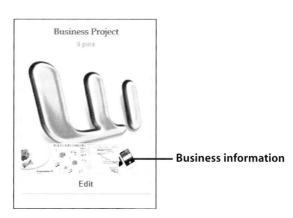

— **Business information**

Sharing Classroom Information

Pinterest's collaborative pinboards are proving quite valuable within the education environment. Educators and students alike are using Pinterest to share and organize essential information.

Many teachers are using Pinterest to post their class syllabus, as well as additional course resources. Pinboards are also useful in hosting supplemental material for a class. You can use Pinterest to post information relevant to the classes you teach and then share those pins with your students. For example, if you're teaching an art class, you can post images from the artists you're studying this semester.

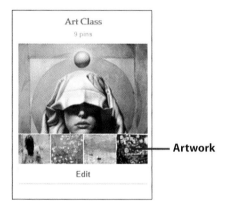

Likewise, you can open a collaborative board to your students, and encourage them to share images and information they find on their own. For example, if you're teaching about dinosaurs, you can create a dinosaur-themed collaborative board and ask students to pin images of dinosaurs they find on the Web. This opens a wealth of new information to both your students and yourself.

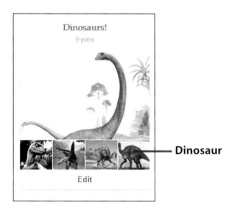

It's Not All Good

KEEP IT PRIVATE

You should never, at any time, encourage students to post their own private images or information on Pinterest or any other social networking site. Instead, take this opportunity to teach your students about online privacy and how most private information should never be made public.

Finally, teachers can find a plethora of education-related resources on Pinterest by browsing the Education category. Just go to the Pinterest home page, mouse over Everything on the navigation bar, and click Education. You'll discover many useful pins from teachers just like you.

Education pin

Sharing with Other Teachers

You can also use Pinterest to share information with fellow educators. Many teachers are using Pinterest to share lesson plans, group projects, and other classroom resources.

Collaborating with Pinterest

A collaborative Pinterest board is very useful for working on group projects. Beyond cataloging basic research, different members of the group can pin items of value to the project—and thus ease the collaborative process.

Collaborating on Business Projects

When it comes to group projects, Pinterest can do more than just organize research articles. You can also use Pinterest to share ideas for the project, as well as pieces of the project itself.

For example, if your group is working on a presentation, you can pin working visuals for the presentation to your group pinboard. That might mean pinning sample images, charts, even slide layouts—anything essential to the completion of the presentation.

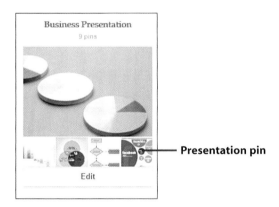

— **Presentation pin**

If your project is more file-based (an accounting project, for example), you can upload your working files to a cloud server (such as Google Docs) and then pin the file's web page to your Pinterest board. This centralizes access to all your documents in one place; it's easy enough to click through the pin to work on the document itself.

Collaborating on School Projects

Pinterest is particularly suited for collaborating on classroom projects. Just about any group project you encounter can be centralized on a Pinterest pinboard.

It starts with the sharing of ideas for a project. As you find items that might be of use or interest to group members, pin them to a collaborative pinboard. Before long, all members of your group will be using Pinterest to bounce ideas off one another.

You can then proceed to sharing project resources via Pinterest. These can be images or videos for a presentation, relevant quotes from online articles, or even more detailed files posted to a file-sharing site. Any item you post to Pinterest is immediately available to the other group members, no matter where they are at the moment.

GET NOTIFIED

To get the most use out of a collaborative pinboard, you need to configure Pinterest to notify you when new pins are made to the board. You do this by clicking the Change Email Settings button on the Edit Profile page. When the Email Settings page appears, make sure that the Group Pins and Comments switches are both clicked "on."

A scrapbooking pinboard

In this chapter, you learn how to create your own Pinterest scrapbooks.

→ Create your own picture scrapbooks
→ Gain inspiration and ideas from fellow Pinterest users

Using Pinterest for Scrapbooking

Pinterest is popular among various types of users, but it holds particular interest for scrapbookers. It helps, of course, that Pinterest itself is a giant scrapbook, with users pinning pictures to pinboards much as scrapbookers glue pictures to scrapbook pages. In fact, pinning to Pinterest is just as easy as—if not easier than—creating a physical scrapbook page.

It's not surprising, then, to find that scrapbookers of all types are adopting Pinterest for their digital scrapbooking needs. Pinterest is also a great place to get inspiration for your scrapbooking projects, whether physical or digital. There's a lot of interesting things going on there.

Creating Your Own Picture Scrapbooks on Pinterest

Scrapbooking is a great way to preserve your personal and family history. It's fun to pull out an old scrapbook to see what everyone looked like and was doing years ago.

Traditional scrapbooking has been around for a long time—since fifteenth century England, as a matter of fact. You assemble a scrapbooking album, consisting of a multi-ring binder and blank pages, and then paste interesting items—photos, newspaper articles, recipes, and so forth—onto the pages. More advanced scrapbookers embrace sophisticated page templates, and collect all sort of items, including report cards, menus, and various found objects. It's a popular hobby; more than four million women in the U.S. alone identify themselves as avid scrapbookers.

With the advent of the personal computer and the Internet, so-called digital scrapbooking came to the fore. Now scrapbookers can create virtual scrapbooks, either on their own PCs or online, containing digital photographs, scanned documents, and the like. Online digital scrapbooks can be easily shared with friends and family, just by sharing a link to a particular web page.

All of which brings us to Pinterest. The scrapbooking community has embraced Pinterest in a big way, which isn't surprising given Pinterest's design that mimics that of a scrapbook page. It's not difficult to envision a Pinterest pinboard as a scrapbook album, devoted to collecting and journaling a particular timeframe, activity, or event.

In a way, Pinterest has reinvented the traditional scrapbook. Instead of using paper and photo prints, you create pinboards to which you pin your collected images. It's just another way to store and share your memories, online.

How can you use Pinterest to create your own digital scrapbooks? There are a number of ways to proceed.

First, you can use Pinterest to document major events and activities in your life. For example, if your oldest child has a birthday party, you can upload pictures from that party to a special Pinterest board. (Name the board "Collin's Fourth Birthday" or something similar.) Share the URL of this board with your friends and family (via email) and everyone gets to share your "scrapbook" of the event, online. No more photo prints to order, no more scrapbooking supplies to purchase or physical scrapbook pages to assemble, nothing to pack and mail to interested parties. It's all online, posted once for everyone to view and enjoy.

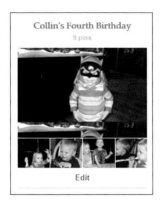

Another approach is to devote a pinboard to a given timeframe, whether that be a month or a year in the life of your family. Name it "Smith Family 2012" and pin all your photos and related images for the year to that pinboard. Naturally, you keep adding new pins to the board as the year progresses; by the end of the year, you have a visual collection of your life events for that time period.

You can also use Pinterest to journal the life of a given individual. In this instance, you might create pinboards for all your children or grandchildren, and pin the appropriate items to each board. You end up with a collection of photos and memorabilia that document the life of each child, from birth to now.

If you've already created digital scrapbooks elsewhere on the Web, you can still pin those pages to Pinterest. Just go to each scrapbook page and pin it to a given pinboard. Create one board for each digital album and then make each page in the album a separate pin. Anyone clicking on your pins will be taken to the original scrapbook page, online and full size.

Scrapbook page

Repinned onto Scrapbook
pages from google.com

Likewise, you can pin individual pages of an existing physical scrapbook to Pinterest. Just scan each page of the album separately and upload the scans as pins to a given pinboard. This way you get to keep your physical scrapbook, with all the effort you put into it, and share it online, as well.

Following Other Scrapbookers for Inspiration

Scrapbookers often form strong social networks with others in the hobby. Those networks can be enhanced by following one another on Pinterest.

To that end, many scrapbookers use Pinterest for inspiration and new ideas. You can learn a lot from the other scrapbookers who use Pinterest.

Many scrapbookers create their own digital scrapbooks on Pinterest, of course. Others like to pin favorite templates, designs, artwork, and the like that can then be used by other scrapbookers. For example, if you find a pinned template you like, just click through to the original web page to access the full-size template.

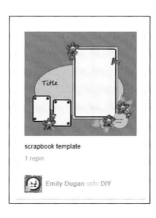

scrapbook template

1 repin

Emily Dugan onto DIY

When you find a pinned item of particular interest, it's a snap to repin it to one of your own pinboards. Create one or more boards to house these inspirational items and then return to the boards for future inspiration.

How can you find fellow scrapbookers to follow on Pinterest? Start by searching Pinterest for the keywords **scrapbook** and **scrapbooking**. (They return slightly different results.) Be sure to look at the search results for both individual pins and boards related to those keywords.

Filter the search results by people and you'll see a number of Pinterest users who claim scrapbooking as an interest. Click through to view these people's pinboards; you'll find lots of folks you might want to follow.

You can also search Pinterest for your favorite scrapbooking stores and supply companies. Many scrapbooking stores are already on Pinterest and have lots of followers; you'll typically find lots of inspiration from these stores online.

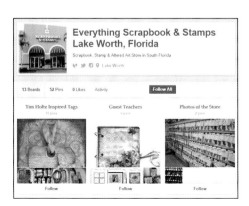

Finally, check out these popular scrapbookers on Pinterest. I'm sure they won't mind gaining a few more followers from the readers of this book!

- Daily Digi (www.pinterest.com/dailydigi/)

- Diana C (www.pinterest.com/lonelyscrapper/)

- Islandmom (www.pinterest.com/islandmomsteph/)

- Katie Nelson the Scrapbook Lady (www.pinterest.com/ktscrapbooklady/)

- Kim de Smet (www.pinterest.com/kim_desmet/)

- Kristin (www.pinterest.com/kleitow/)

- Marisa Lerin (www.pinterest.com/marisalerin/)

- Scrappin Bunnies LLC (www.pinterest.com/scrappinbunnies/)

- Scrappymo! (www.pinterest.com/scrappymo/)

- Sweet Shoppe Designs (www.pinterest.com/ssdpins/)

REPINNING BOARDS

If you find yourself repinning a lot of ideas from fellow scrapbookers, you'll want to create multiple pinboards for these items. Consider separate boards for templates/layouts, embellishments, sketches, ideas, and so forth. You might even want to create different boards for different approaches, such as birthdays, events, and so on.

A photography pinboard

In this chapter, you learn how photographers can best use Pinterest.

→ Find out whether Pinterest is good or bad for photographers

→ Learn how to share photos on Pinterest

→ Discover how to use Pinterest for wedding photography

→ Learn how to gain inspiration from other photos on Pinterest

Using Pinterest for Photographers

Pinterest is a visual social networking site, which means that people pin a lot of photographs to their pinboards. This focus on digital photos makes Pinterest an interesting site for both amateur and professional photographers.

Savvy photographers are learning to use Pinterest to gain more exposure for their work. Other photographers, however, are wary of putting their photos on Pinterest; there are lots of concerns, copyright among them.

If you're a photographer, should you upload your photos to Pinterest or allow them to be pinned? It's an interesting question, and one that photographers everywhere are evaluating.

Is Pinterest Good or Bad for Photographers?

If you're not a professional photographer, you might naively think that Pinterest is a good thing for the photography profession. After all, a photographer need only upload her photos to gain a potential audience in the millions. What's not to like about that?

To the professional photographer, it comes down to a question of exposure versus control. Yes, a photo pinned to a Pinterest board can gain a lot of viewers, but that doesn't necessarily translate into new business. In fact, a pinned photo could very well be used without the photographer's consent—or adequate compensation.

In other words, the situation is complicated.

Why Some Photographers Are Wary of Pinterest

Surprisingly to some, many photographers are quite negative about displaying their work on the Pinterest site. What concerns do these photographers have about Pinterest?

There are actually several concerns, ranging from the quality of the displayed images to the risk of copyright violation.

First, there's the image quality thing. Pinterest image thumbnails might not be the best way to view many photographs. It's a simple matter of size; details that contribute to the overall effect in a full-size photograph might simply be lost in a typical Pinterest thumbnail.

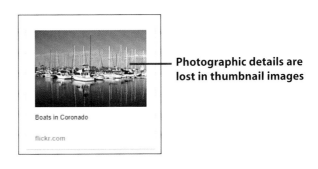

Photographic details are lost in thumbnail images

Boats in Coronado

flickr.com

And it's not much better when you click to enlarge an item; Pinterest's expanded pin images are only 900 pixels high by 600 pixels wide, maximum. A dedicated photographer might not want his images to be viewed at that low resolution, and he might prefer that people view them in higher resolution on his own website.

Uploaded Images

If you link to an image on another website, the 900 x 600 pixel image is as good as it gets on the Pinterest site. If, however, you upload an image from your computer to a pinboard, anyone clicking the expanded pin image will see the picture at its original (presumably larger) size.

Some photographers might question the demographics of the typical Pinterest user, and whether Pinterest is really a good match for serious photography. Yes, there are a lot of people interested in crafts and fashion on Pinterest, but also a lot of people interested in the arts. That translates into a lot of photography lovers on the site.

The most serious concerns, however, relate to ownership and control of the images in question. Photographers are naturally concerned about maintaining control over their own intellectual property; they wish to be properly compensated for the use of said images.

In terms of control, the first concern comes from where the images are hosted. When an item is pinned to Pinterest, it doesn't change the website where the picture is originally hosted. However, Pinterest does create copies of the image to use as thumbnail images and expanded images on its own website. So right there, you have an issue of control when copies of copyrighted images are hosted on Pinterest, outside the photographer's control.

Beyond that, images posted on Pinterest could be reused without the original photographer's knowledge or permission. Granted, the reuse would be of a lower resolution version, but the issue remains. There is nothing Pinterest currently does to restrict usage of the images pinned to its site.

There is also the question of whether a given photographer approves of individuals pinning his images to the Pinterest site, without explicit permission. What some might see as free exposure and promotion, others might see as unwanted exposure and unauthorized use. (These same photographers are likely to complain about their copyrighted images appearing in Google image search results, too.)

Terms of Use

Learn more about Pinterest's terms of use and how they affect copyright in Appendix A, "Understanding Pinterest's Terms of Use" (online).

In this regard, some photographers view Pinterest as an enabler of illegal activity, much the same way the original Napster was to the music industry in the 1990s. These photographers view the very act of pinning one of their images as copyright infringement. Their work is being displayed without their knowledge or consent, which might be a violation of copyright.

It may be a matter of degree, but that degree matters. Pinterest's latest terms of service state that by making content available to the site, a member grants to Cold Brew Labs (Pinterest's owning company) a "non-exclusive, royalty-free, transferrable, sublicensable, worldwide license to use, display, reproduce, re-pin, modify (e.g., re-format), re-arrange, and distribute" that content. That's a lot, but it does stop short of saying that Pinterest can actually resell your content, which the site's original terms of service said. The new terms of service clarifies the fact that Pinterest isn't interested in selling your photography, just in displaying it.

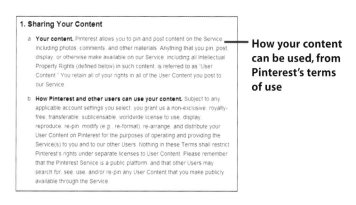

How your content can be used, from Pinterest's terms of use

Still, some professional photographers think that Pinterest is taking too many liberties with their intellectual property. In response, some have removed Pin It buttons from their websites, and enabled the "no pin" code to keep Pinterest from pinning their images.

No Pin Code

Learn how to keep your images from being pinned in Chapter 14, "Adding Pin It Buttons to Your Website or Blog."

Are These Concerns Justified?

Some of these concerns are justified; others are not.

In terms of the image-quality concern, it's true that images on the Pinterest site are of rather low resolution. But that's not the way all users view images on Pinterest; when clicked, users are taken to the hosting website, where the image can be viewed at its original resolution. In other words, think of the thumbnail and pin as just links to the original photograph.

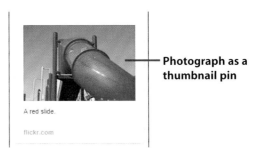

Photograph as a thumbnail pin

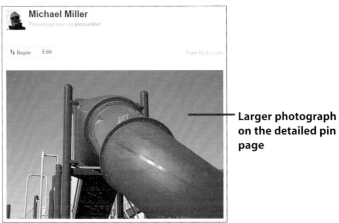

Larger photograph on the detailed pin page

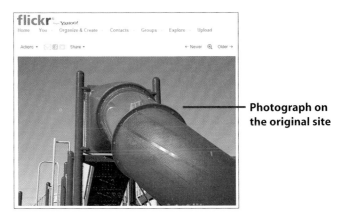

Photograph on the original site

As to the demographics concern, it's true that Pinterest primarily appeals to females between the ages of 25 to 54. If that's a photographer's target audience, great; if not, then Pinterest might not be a perfect match—at least not yet.

You see, social networks evolve over time. Facebook, for example, was originally targeted at college students, and only recently has expanded its reach to include an older and more affluent audience. It's possible, if not likely, that Pinterest will expand its user base to be more in sync with that of the audience for professional photography. So you can't really say that Pinterest is a waste of time for professional photographers; that's simply not the case.

The argument about losing control of an image because a copy exists on the Pinterest site is somewhat disingenuous. The Internet itself is a series of links and digital copies; you see copies of images every time you do a Google image search. Just because a copy of your copyrighted image is hosted on another site, whether that be Pinterest or Google, the original copyright is not negated. The image belongs to the original copyright holder, wherever a copy of that image is hosted. Think of the Pinterest pin as a referral to the copyrighted image on the original site.

In terms of exposing an image to unauthorized use, if you accept that the image pinned to the Pinterest site is acceptable, the concern is really about third parties copying the enlarged pin image for use in some commercial endeavor—an advertisement, perhaps, or maybe a magazine article. Now, some of this exposure might fall under the terms of fair use, such as when a critic comments on a given work and is thus free to quote from the work itself. Pure commercial exploitation is another thing, and one that the copyright holder continues to have control over. No one can make money by selling a copyrighted image without prior authorization from and appropriate compensation to the copyright holder. Nothing that Pinterest does changes that; in fact, it's Pinterest's stated intent *not* to take advantage of user content in that fashion.

WATERMARKS

One way to keep a copyrighted image from being illegally used is to place a watermark on the image. This is simply a word or phrase (typically something like "Property of *copyright holder*") that is placed over the image. Not only does the watermark make the claim for the copyright holder, it makes the image virtually unusable for commercial purposes. (Anyone purchasing the image for commercial use receives a pristine version of the photo, sans watermark.)

Watermark on a photograph

Beyond all this, photographers have the option of making their images unpinnable (by including a "no pin" code, as previously discussed) or asking Pinterest to remove any copyrighted images they don't want to appear on the site. Pinterest is extremely friendly toward copyright holders and removes unauthorized images when requested.

Removing Unauthorized Images

Learn more about reporting unauthorized use of copyrighted images in Chapter 12, "Learning Pinterest Etiquette."

Potential Benefits to Photographers

All previous concerns aside, Pinterest offers some obvious benefits to both amateur and professional photographers. If nothing else, having one of your photos pinned exposes it to a much wider audience than would have seen it otherwise.

Some photographers are overly protective of their work. Others want their work to be seen. A photograph hanging on your wall or stored on your computer enriches no one but yourself; a photograph shared with the world brings joy to many others. It's still your photograph, but now others can enjoy it, as well.

For many photographers, that's where Pinterest comes in. Like dedicated photo-sharing sites, Pinterest lets you aggregate all your favorite images in topic-oriented pinboards. When others visit your boards, they get to enjoy your photographs—and, if they like, link back to your professional website to see more and possibly make a purchase or engage your services. In this way, Pinterest both showcases your work and promotes your business.

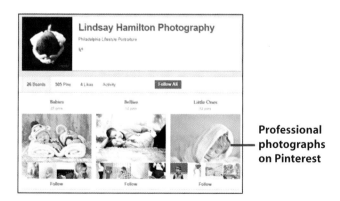

Professional photographs on Pinterest

In fact, many professional photographers view Pinterest as a great promotional tool. Not only do you get to highlight samples of your work, potential clients get to peruse your photos and other pins for ideas they'd like you to implement. It's a win-win for both photographers and their clients.

Even if you're not a professional photographer, Pinterest is still useful for showcasing the pictures you take. Whether you have a bunch of holiday pics to share with your family or some more creative photos you'd like to show around, Pinterest makes it easy to highlight your photographs on dedicated pinboards, for free. You can either upload your digital photos or pin photos already uploaded to another website.

And remember, just because you pin a photo to Pinterest doesn't mean you give up any of your creative rights. Pinterest doesn't gain copyright to a photo just because it's pinned to the site; you, the original photographer, remain in creative control. The only difference is that you've now gained additional exposure for that photo, thanks to Pinterest. (And if someone repins a photo you've posted… well, that's just more eyeballs for your work.)

Should You Pin Your Photographs?

The question still remains—should you or shouldn't you pin your photographs to Pinterest?

There isn't a single right answer to this question. Some photographers find Pinterest useful for gaining more exposure for their work. Others don't want that exposure, at least not with the attendant risk to their copyrighted works.

Many foresighted photographers, especially wedding photographers, recognize that Pinterest is a visual medium with appeal to an attractive demographic (women between the ages of 25 and 44). Because they're in a visual business, Pinterest becomes a go-to site to display and promote their portfolios.

The reality is that Pinterest can drive a lot of business to professional photographers. For example, pro photographer Trey Ratcliff (www.stuckincustoms.com) relies on word of mouth advertising for his business, and finds that 15% of the traffic to his website comes directly from Pinterest. That's free promotion (nothing spent but his time) for a significant boost in potential customers.

Other photographers use Pinterest as a place to post visual inspirations for their clients. It's a way of saying "here's an approach you might find interesting—we can try that." Pinterest, then, becomes a database of creative ideas to inspire both clients and photographers.

Of course, if you want to maintain complete control over your work, Pinterest may not be for you. When you pin a photograph to one of your boards, there is nothing to keep others from repinning it on theirs. That doesn't give them ownership of the image, mind you, but does take viewership out of your immediate control. It's also possible that someone might reuse a photograph you pin, even at its compromised resolution. You could sue the unauthorized user, of course, but why open the door to copyright abuse?

To answer the question of whether or not to use Pinterest, you have to weigh the pros and cons and make your own personal decision. It's certainly possible for photographers to avoid Pinterest (and to use the "no follow" code to keep their photos from being pinned), but in doing so you might forfeit a potentially significant source of new clients.

Sharing Your Photographs on Pinterest

Whether you're a professional photographer serious about growing your client base, or an amateur picture taker wanting to share some holiday snaps, Pinterest is the place to do it. Creative use of Pinterest pinboards can result in increased awareness of your work.

Pinning Your Photos

There are two ways to pin photos to Pinterest—pinning existing pages or uploading new pins.

The first approach lets you pin a link to a photo that's already visible on the Web. This assumes, of course, that you've already uploaded the picture to another website. This can be your own professional website or blog, or it can a traditional photo-sharing site, such as Flickr. This approach is relatively easy; all you have to do is navigate to the photo in question, click the Pin It button in your web browser's toolbar, and select which board you want to pin to. There's no new uploading required.

The second approach does not require you to have previously uploaded a photo to the Web. Instead, you click Add in the Pinterest navigation bar and then click Upload a Pin. Select the photo to upload, select which board to upload to, and Pinterest does the rest.

Uploading and Pinning Photos
Learn more about the different ways to pin a photo in Chapter 6, "Pinning to Pinterest."

Pinning an existing photo from Flickr

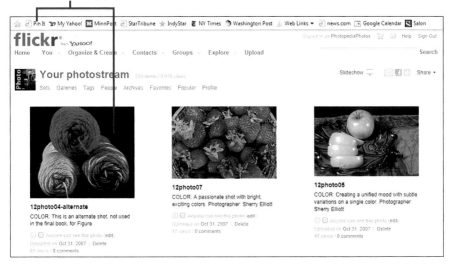

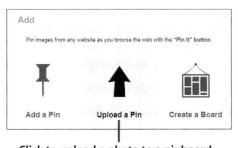

Click to upload a photo to a pinboard

The benefit of this second approach is that when someone clicks the pin thumbnail, the photograph gets displayed at a higher resolution. The main issue with this approach is that clicking the photo does not automatically take viewers back to your website. In fact, clicking the photo does nothing—unless you manually add a URL link to the pin.

To do this, you first have to upload the photo as previously described then go to that pin and click the Edit button. When the Edit Pin page displays, the Link box is empty; enter the URL for your website or blog into this box then click the red Save Pin button. Now visitors go to your site when they click the image.

Edit Pin

Description	Hayley at sunset.
Link		────── Enter your website URL here
Board	Photography ▾
Delete	Delete Pin

Save Pin

Whether you pin an existing photo or upload a new one, make sure you add detailed descriptions to each pin. Describe what's in the photo and maybe even give the details of the image itself—exposure setting, lens used, lighting, that sort of thing. If you're a pro, present yourself accordingly.

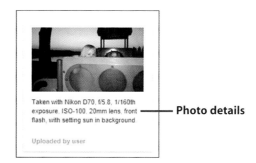

Taken with Nikon D70, f/5.8, 1/160th exposure, ISO-100, 20mm lens, front flash, with setting sun in background. ──── **Photo details**

Uploaded by user

Organizing Your Pinboards

Key to sharing photos on Pinterest is proper organization of your pinboards. You don't want to lump all your photographs in a single "pictures" board; you want to create separate boards for different types of photographs.

Here are some ideas on the types of boards you can create:

- Portraits
- Wedding photos
- Family photos
- Sports
- Holidays

- Action photos
- Product photos
- Landscapes
- Nature
- Creative shots

The underlying advice here is to group your photos by theme. Put all like photos together in a single pinboard, and differentiate your pinboards by topic or type of picture. Separate portraits and other photos of people from landscapes and other nature photographs. Make it easy for your followers (and potential clients) to find the types of photos they're looking for.

How Wedding Photographers Can Take Advantage of Pinterest

Wedding photos make up a key subset of the larger photography category. Wedding photographers are finding Pinterest particularly useful for both promoting their businesses and helping them interact with their clients.

The first thing to know is that your clients are already using Pinterest. Brides are utilizing the site to gain inspiration for their weddings, as well as to identify items for their wedding registries. If someone is planning a wedding, chances are they're quite familiar with Pinterest before they even contact you.

Building on this familiarity, Pinterest can help you visually connect with your clients. The most obvious way to do this is to direct your clients to your Pinterest boards to view samples of your previous work. Create different boards for different types of wedding photos—modern weddings, rustic weddings, outdoor weddings, and the like.

Wedding photography pinboards

You can also repin work from other photographers, in an "ideas and inspirations" board, to help get the creative flow going. In addition, you can create a collaborative pinboard for each client and encourage the client to pin photos there that they like. This way you can share your clients' inspiration and get a better handle on the types of shots they'd like to see.

Collaborative Pinboards

Learn more about creating collaborative pinboards in Chapter 17, "Using Pinterest for Sharing and Collaboration."

ENCOURAGING IDEAS FROM CLIENTS

The concept of using Pinterest to encourage input from your clients isn't limited to wedding photography. Any professional photographer can ask a client to pin images they find interesting or appealing and then use those images to create new shots for the client. The best way to do this is to create a collaborative pinboard where both you and the client can pin. People who have trouble describing what they want in words, but can more easily point to visual examples of what they like. Pinterest is ideal for that.

Following Other Photographers for Inspiration

Pinterest is also of interest of photographers looking for inspiration. There are a lot of photographers on the Pinterest site, and a lot of beautiful and interesting photographs posted. It's a great place to find photographs you might wish to emulate in your own fashion.

When you're browsing Pinterest for ideas, it's best to repin the most interesting shots on your own boards. In fact, you might want to create multiple boards for different types of ideas. You can create boards for photos that inspire you, places you'd like to shoot, interesting props, effective lighting, and the like.

One good place to look for inspirational photos is the Best of Pinterest Photographers board, located at www.pinterest.com/farbspiel/best-of-pinterest-photographers/. This board represents a visual catalog of some of the best photographers using the Pinterest site.

Best of Pinterest Photographers board

Of course, you should also browse Pinterest's general Photography category. Go to the Pinterest home page, mouse over Everything in the filter, and click Photography. All properly tagged photographs are displayed here.

Pinterest's Photography category

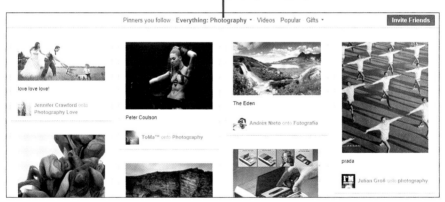

Pinterest pins can make interesting blog posts

Pinterest for Bloggers

Repinned onto Infographics
from google.co.uk

In this chapter, you learn how to integrate Pinterest into your existing blog.

→ Discover why Pinterest is important to bloggers
→ Learn how to connect your blog to Pinterest
→ Find out how to share blog posts on Pinterest
→ Discover how to embed pins in your blog posts
→ Learn how to make your blog posts more pinnable

Using Pinterest for Bloggers

Even though Pinterest is still in its formative days, it has already gained a huge following among bloggers. Many bloggers find Pinterest useful for attracting new blog readers, as well as expanding the reach of their blogs. Pinterest can also serve as the source of inspiration for future blog posts.

If you're a blogger, how can you use Pinterest in conjunction with your blog? It's a short jump from a Pinterest pinboard to the blogosphere—all you have to do is make it!

Why Pinterest Is Important for Your Blog

Pinterest is fast becoming an important vehicle driving blog traffic. By February 2012, Pinterest was driving more traffic to blogs than Twitter—which is pretty impressive given Pinterest's 11 million users versus Twitter's 100 million plus users. That means Pinterest users are more engaged than Twitter followers and have interests that parallel those of many blog readers.

Traffic Drivers

Google's search engine remains the dominant driver of blog traffic, accounting for 48% of all referral traffic, according to Shareaholic. (Facebook accounts for 6% of referral traffic; Pinterest for a little more than 1%; Twitter for about 0.8%.)

This correlation between Pinterest users and blog visitors has a lot to do with the types of topics blogged about. Blogs that focus on women's lifestyle, home décor, arts and crafts, and food have been the biggest beneficiaries of the Pinterest boom. These are the most frequently pinned subjects on Pinterest and are the topics of many of the most popular blogs.

Connecting Your Blog to Pinterest

If you're a blogger, you want to take advantage of this newfound interest. To that end, you need to connect your blog to your Pinterest account in as many ways as feasible.

Use Consistent Profiles

The first order of business is to present a consistent image in all your online activities. That means using the same profile photo for your blog and your Pinterest account, as well as using a similar description of yourself on both your blog and Pinterest. You're the same person no matter where you post, and your profiles should reflect this.

Profile picture ——— Michael Miller / Profile description

Add a Pinterest Follow Button to Your Blog

You want your blog followers to be able to find and follow you on Pinterest. The easiest way to do this is to add a Pinterest Follow button to your blog. This should typically go in your blog's sidebar so it's visible however people are reading your blog.

 ─ **Follow button**

Adding Buttons

Learn how to add Follow and Pin It buttons in Chapter 14, "Adding Pin It Buttons to Your Website or Blog."

Add Pin It Buttons to Individual Blog Posts

You want to encourage your blog readers to pin your content to Pinterest. The most effective way to do this is to add Pin It buttons to each blog post you make. Anyone clicking this button is led step-by-step through the pinning process on the Pinterest site.

Pin It button ─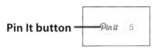

Although you can add Pin It buttons manually to each post, assuming you know how to edit the underlying HTML code, some blogging sites make it easier for you to perform this task. For example, if you use WordPress to host your blog, there are several plug-ins available for adding Pin It buttons, including the following:

- Pin It on Pinterest (www.wordpress.org/extend/plugins/pin-it-on-pinterest/)
- Pinterest "Pin It" Button (www.wordpress.org/extend/plugins/pinterest-pin-it-button/)
- Pinterest Pin It Button (www.wordpress.org/extend/plugins/pinterest/)

It's Not All Good

PIN TO PERMALINKS

You want to encourage your blog's readers to pin to specific blog posts by using each post's permalink. If they pin to your blog's home page (which can happen if you include Pin It button in your blog template) each pin links back to your main blog, not to the appropriate post.

Link to Your Blog from Your Pinterest Profile

Finally, you want to link to your blog from your Pinterest profile. You do this by mousing over your name on the Pinterest navigation bar and selecting Edit Profile. When the Edit Profile page appears, scroll to the Website box and enter the URL of your blog. Click the red Save Profile button and a new button displays in your Pinterest profile. Anyone clicking this button is taken to your blog.

Website/blog button 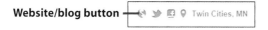 Twin Cities, MN

Sharing Blog Posts and Pictures on Pinterest

Another effective way to promote your blog is to pin content and images from your blog to one of your Pinterest pinboards. Anyone clicking the pin goes directly to that specific blog post.

Pinning Images from Your Blog

The key is to identify interesting images in your blog posts, and then pin those images to the appropriate Pinterest board. Remember to pin the permalinks to individual posts rather than pinning back to your blog's main page.

Blog image pinned
to a pinboard

From my blog

Pinned onto Parenting and
Grandparenting from
mikeandsherrypictures.blogspot.com

When you pin your own blog posts, consider *where* you pin them to. If you don't pin a lot of items, you can create a single pinboard for your blog, named after the blog. For example, if your blog is called Pretty Food, you might name the associated pinboard Pretty Food Blog.

If you pin a lot of posts, you'll find that you quickly overpopulate a single pinboard. To that end, you might create different pinboards for different blog topics or keywords. For example, instead of pinning to a general Pretty Food Blog board, you might have individual boards for Appetizers, Main Courses, Dessert, and so forth.

Pin Appealing Images

Whatever you pin from your blog, make sure it's a visually appealing image. Pinterest is all about the visuals, and if the images you choose don't cut it, no one will view or repin them.

Using a Pinterest Board as a Blog Roll

You can also create a Pinterest board that replicates the blog roll on your blog site. A blog roll is a list of those blogs you like and follow; it's easy enough to create a Blog Roll pinboard and pin images from your favorite blogs there. Anyone clicking on a blog roll pin is taken to that blog.

When you create blog roll pins, you probably want to pin to the blog's main page rather than to any specific blog post. Make sure the pin's URL points to the blog's main address.

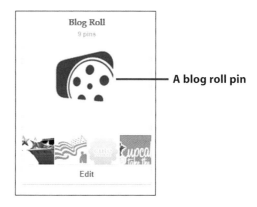

A blog roll pin

Using Pins in Your Blog Posts

Connecting Pinterest to your blog goes both ways. Not only can you pin your blog posts to Pinterest, you can also embed pins—from you and from other users—in your blog posts.

It's easy enough to do this. When you find a particular pin worthy of mentioning in your blog, click the pin's thumbnail to display the expanded pin page. Click the Embed button then copy the embed code into a new blog post.

The embedded pin not only includes the pinned image, but it also credits the pinner and the original source of the image. This information is important; you always want to credit the original source.

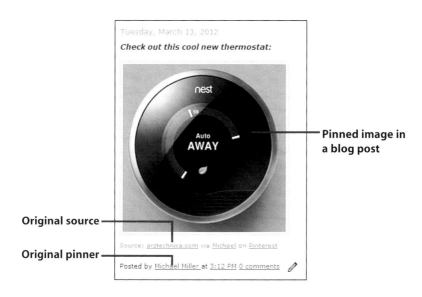

Pinned image in a blog post

Original source

Original pinner

How to Get Your Blog Posts Pinned—and Repinned

One of the key aspects of promoting your blog via Pinterest is to encourage your blog readers to pin your posts to Pinterest. This isn't as easy as it sounds.

Creating Pinnable Posts

The first step in encouraging others to pin your posts is to make sure you have pinnable content. That means that the post needs to be about something useful or interesting to the reader so that the reader is inspired to share it.

It also means using an appealing image in the post. Remember, Pinterest is a visual social network, so if you don't have any visuals in a post, no one will pin it. You need to include eye-popping images that look good at a smaller thumbnail size—images that your readers will want to share.

Making It Easy to Pin

As discussed previously, you need to make it as easy as possible for your readers to pin your blog posts. Don't rely on each and every reader having a Pin It button installed in her web browser; embed a Pin It button in every blog post you make.

Discovering What Others Have Pinned from Your Blog

After you start integrating Pinterest with your blog, you'll soon be curious about just which images people are pinning. You can find out what's being pinned by entering the following URL into your web browser:

www.pinterest.com/source/*yourblog.com*

Replace ***yourblog.com*** with the full URL of your blog. Pinterest displays all the recent items pinned from your blog. Each pin includes the user who pinned it, and which board she pinned it to.

Pinned blog posts —

Nordstrom's brand pinboard

Nordstrom

We're a fashion specialty retailer of clothing, shoes & accessories. Cust Service 1-888-282-6060. Social team: Lily, Kent, Katie and Bryan

Seattle, WA

| 33 Boards | 511 Pins | 2 Likes | Activity | **Follow All** |

Prom Inspiration at Nord...
29 pins

Spring Trend: Nautical V...
13 pins

The Nordstrom Thread B...
30 pins

Follow   Follow   Follow

21

→ Examining whether to promote your business with Pinterest
→ Discovering how other businesses are using Pinterest
→ Getting your business up and running on Pinterest
→ Discovering tips for more effective marketing with Pinterest
→ Learning how to measure your Pinterest success

Using Pinterest to Market Your Business

As you now know, individuals are increasingly embracing Pinterest to share visual items online. This rapid growth is also attracting a lot of businesses to the party.

Should you consider using Pinterest to market your business? There are a lot of good reasons to do so, not the least of which is that lots of businesses are already using Pinterest—and having good success. It's all a matter of knowing what to market on Pinterest, and how.

Should You Use Pinterest to Promote Your Business?

Pinterest certainly has appeal to certain types of consumers. Does that popularity translate to businesses?

In other words, should you use Pinterest to promote your business?

For many types of businesses, the answer is an unqualified yes. Pinterest offers a unique new way to promote your business and engage with your target customers. And you can do all that without spending a ton of money.

As you've learned, Pinterest is experiencing unprecedented growth, especially among women aged 24 to 54. That's an attractive demographic for many types of businesses—not that the increasingly large number of potential customers isn't attractive in and of itself. That's tens of millions of potential customers, growing larger each month, most of whom are predisposed to looking at pretty images of things that are important to them.

We've already seen that Pinterest successfully drives large amounts of traffic to blogs and other sites connected with pinned items. That means Pinterest can also drive traffic back to your website, if you pin items with particular customer appeal.

The benefits, then, of using Pinterest to market your business include the following:

- Rapidly increasing popularity
- Attractive demographics
- Proven ability to drive traffic to other sites
- Appeal in specific vertical markets

Should your business market with Pinterest? Yes—especially if you offer products or services targeted to Pinterest's core customer base.

HOW STABLE IS PINTEREST?

You don't want to invest your marketing funds in a website that might not be around a year from now. Fortunately Pinterest, while a relative newcomer to the social networking scene, looks to be around for the long haul. The company is remarkably well funded, having received a second round of funding (for $27 million) in October 2011. The company is valued at around $200 million.

As to how Pinterest generates revenue, you might be surprised at the lack of advertising on the Pinterest site. That's because, unlike Facebook and other social networks, Pinterest doesn't make its money from advertising. Instead, Pinterest generates revenues by functioning as an affiliate marketer when people click through and purchase pinned items from online retailers. That is, Pinterest receives a commission when someone clicks an item pinned on the Pinterest site to go to a retailer's site and purchase that item. It's an unconventional way for a large website to make money, but it appears to be working for Pinterest.

How Businesses Are Using Pinterest Today

Given everything that Pinterest is today, it's not surprising that the site is attracting a lot of interest from the business community. Whether you work for a small business or a large corporation, Pinterest has a lot to offer—not the least of which is a large impact for a relatively low investment.

What Can You Use Pinterest For?

There are many reasons for a business to use Pinterest today. Yes, you can use Pinterest to drive traffic to your company's website, but there's more to it than that.

How can a company benefit from marketing on Pinterest? Here's a short list:

- **Drive traffic and sales.** This is probably the number-one reason for most businesses to use Pinterest. You pin items to your company's pinboards in the hope that potential customers will click on those pins, be taken to your own website, and eventually purchase either what they were looking at or something else.

- **Provide product information**. It may be that you're more interested in providing product information to potential customers, with the expectations that sales conversion will happen later. In that case, use your pinned items to link back to product information pages on your site.

- **Highlight events and activities.** You're not limited to pinning product photos. You can also pin photos and videos of past and upcoming company events—new store openings, community projects, you name it. It's a great way to keep your customers informed of what's going on with your company.

- **Engage with customers**. In spite of all the images, Pinterest is, at heart, a social network—and social networks are all about engagement. To this end, you can use Pinterest to build a community around your brand or products. Encourage customers to repin your items and share your pins with all their friends.

- **Improve your website's search rankings**. This one might not be obvious, but it's a real benefit. When someone clicks a pinned image to go to your website, the number of links back to your site increases. If you're at all versed in search engine optimization (SEO), you know that backlinks are one of the key contributors to how high a site ranks on a search results page. The more Pinterest users click back to your site, the higher your site ranks with Google, Bing, and the other search engines.

- **Conduct market research**. You can learn a lot about your customers by looking at what they're pinning. Click through your followers list and examine their pins; you'll get a good idea of what they're interested in at the moment, which is valuable (and free!) market research.

What Types of Businesses Do Well on Pinterest?

To be fair, Pinterest isn't a perfect match for every type of business. Because of the visual nature of the site and the demographic makeup of its customers base, Pinterest is better suited for certain types of businesses than others.

As you might suspect, businesses that offer products and services for women (and their families) are the prime beneficiaries of Pinterest marketing. But these aren't the only types of businesses doing well on Pinterest; some of the more successful types of businesses currently on Pinterest include the following:

- Architecture
- Crafts and hobbies
- Fashion and clothing (women's, men's, and children's)
- Food, beverages, and cooking
- Health care
- Home improvement/DIY
- Interior design and room décor

- Personal care and grooming
- Pets
- Sports
- Technology
- Toys and other children's items
- Travel
- Weddings

Women's shoes from Sarah Riley Shoes (www.pinterest.com/sarahrileyshoes/)

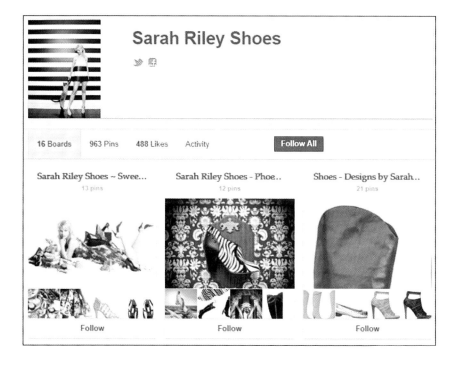

The Home Depot (www.pinterest.com/homedepot/) on Pinterest

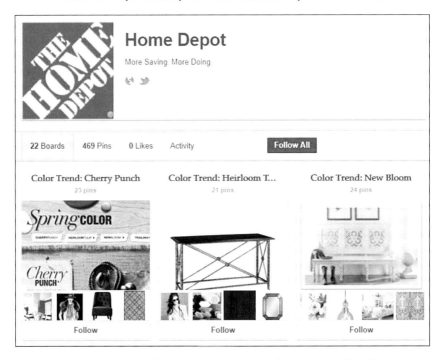

Natural Pet Market (www.pinterest.com/natpetmarket/), an eco-friendly pet store

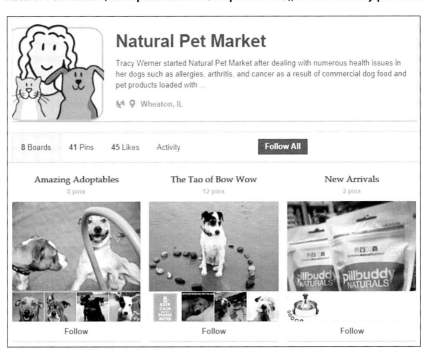

Children's toys from Learning Express Toys (www.pinterest.com/learningexpress/)

Now, these aren't the only businesses profiting from a Pinterest presence, but they give you a sense of what's working and what's not.

Visual Marketing

Pinterest works best if your products or services are visual in nature. You pin images, after all; if you can't present your company or products in pictures, you're probably better off marketing elsewhere.

Getting Your Business Started on Pinterest

Setting up your business on Pinterest is exactly the same as creating a personal Pinterest account. That's because Pinterest doesn't have company or brand accounts; it's exactly the same whether you're a person or representing a company.

Establish a Pinterest Account for Your Company or Brand

Your company's Pinterest presence is anchored to your Pinterest account. That means opening a new Pinterest account for your business—not reusing an existing personal account. Try to snag a username that's close to your company or brand name. And consider different accounts for different brands, lines, or products.

Write a Promotional Profile

After you create your company account, you need to get your copywriters involved in writing the profile description. This needs to be a piece of marketing copy telling customers who you are and what you offer.

Calypso St. Barth's Pinterest profile (www.pinterest.com/calypsostbarth/), complete with vivid promotional description

Calypso St Barth

Over the last 20 years, Calypso St. Barth has grown from a modest French resort-wear line into a global luxury lifestyle brand with a passionate following. The brand offers a no-fuss approach to boho ...

 St Barth

Use Your Company Logo or Product Photo for Your Profile Picture

As for your profile picture, you can go one of two ways. The most obvious approach is to upload your company's logo as your profile picture; it's great branding. But if your Pinterest account is for a specific brand or product, you might want to use a product photo instead.

Coca Cola's Pinterest profile (www.pinterest.com/cocacola/)— the product is the brand is the profile picture

Coca-Cola

Discovering moments of happiness, one picture at a time. Share your moment: http://CokeURL.com/8mux

Atlanta, GA

Link Back to Your Company Website and Other Social Network Accounts

When you complete your account profile, you're encouraged to include a link back to your website. Do. The website button is displayed beneath your profile picture and description; anyone who clicks this button goes directly to your main site.

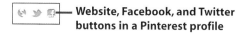 **Website, Facebook, and Twitter buttons in a Pinterest profile**

For that matter, you should also link your Pinterest account to your company's Facebook and Twitter accounts. This cross-posts your Pinterest pins to your other social media, and also displays Facebook and Twitter buttons next to your website button in your profile.

Add a Pinterest Follow Button to Your Website

You want to encourage cross-pollenization between your Pinterest and website presences, which means embedding a Pinterest Follow button on your company's site. Anyone who clicks this button will be taken to your main Pinterest page.

 **A typical Pinterest Follow button**

Create Interesting and Appropriate Pinboards

Now you need to create the pinboards to which you will pin all those interesting items from your website. You want your boards to reflect the different products you offer, and the many ways those products can be used.

So, for example, if you're a shoe retailer, you might create boards for Women's Shoes, Men's Shoes, Athletic Shoes, and the like. Or maybe you create separate boards for each brand you sell. Or, if you sell women's shoes only, you might create boards for High Heels, Pumps, Flats, Boots, Sneakers, and the like. Think of how your customers view or use your products, and create and name your boards accordingly.

**Product-related pinboards from shoe retailer Clog Heaven
(www.pinterest.com/clogheaven/)**

Start Pinning!

After you've created your pinboards, it's time to start filling them up with pins. When you first start out, you want to make an extra effort to populate all your boards with a half-dozen or so pins each (so they look relatively full in thumbnail view), then begin dropping in more pins over time.

How often should you pin? Once or twice a day is probably good; your followers will receive notice of all new pins you make, and you don't want to overwhelm them with too many pins at once. That said, you also don't want to pin so infrequently that your followers forget all about you; anything less than once or twice a week probably isn't enough.

Pin Schedule

It makes sense to establish a constant schedule for your pinning; keep to the schedule and you're doing good. That doesn't mean that you can't post outside your scheduled pins, however. When you have something new and important to share, feel free to pin at will.

And remember, every pin you make needs to (a) link back to your company website and (b) include a marketing-oriented description. Pin about your products and how they're being used; also make sure that you're pinning about things your customers are interested in. The definition of "pinnable" becomes more nuanced when you're talking about attracting new customers and keeping the attention of your existing ones.

Tips for More Effective Marketing with Pinterest

Now that you know the basics of setting up a Pinterest account for your business, let's look at a few additional tips that make your marketing efforts more effective.

Post More Than Just Product Photos

Yes, you should populate your Pinterest boards with pictures of your most popular products. But you need to post more than that. Consider more lifestyle-oriented photos that show your products in use, or photos of other items of interest to your target audience.

Gardening shears in use from Lowes (www.pinterest.com/lowes/)

Knowing the right time to prune is crucial. Pruning at the wrong time typically won't damage plants, but it can sacrifice that year's flowers or fruit.

7 likes 33 repins

lowescreativeideas.com

Create User-Focused Boards

Along the same theme, you should make sure that your pinboards have an obvious user focus. Of course you can (and probably should) create boards around specific product lines, but you should also create boards that focus on how customers use your products.

For example, Williams-Sonoma uses its pinboards to pin links to recipes and other kitchen-related activities. They have boards such as Recipe of the Day, Seafood Suppers, Seasonal Ingredients, Meatless Mains, and the like. It's all very customer focused, as opposed to being company or product focused.

**Williams-Sonoma's (www.pinterest.com/williamssonoma/)
lifestyle-oriented pinboards**

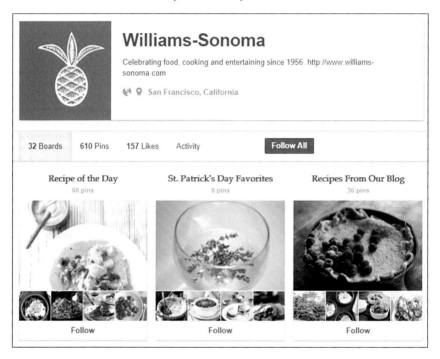

For that matter, consider creating one or more boards with product how-tos, either in image or video form. Use Pinterest's visual format to *show* people how to do important things with your products—or just how to use what you sell.

Owner's Guides Board

Another good idea—create a board with pins to your online owner's manuals and guides, kind of a one-stop shop for customers needing help using your products.

Create an About Us Board

Many customers want to know more about who they're dealing with. To that end, create an "about us" board that tells the story of your company—who you are and what you do. Include behind-the-scenes photos of your offices or factories, top management, key team members, and so forth. It's your opportunity to add a personal face to your company or brand.

The About Us pinboard from The Expressionary (www.pinterest.com/myexpressionary/)

Connect Socially

Remember that Pinterest is a social network and apply the principles you use with your overall social media marketing program. That means establishing a two-way presence on Pinterest, not just one-way communication.

You do this by participating in the following activities:

- Encourage customers to comment on your pins and then respond to those comments.

- Comment on and like other pins of interest to your customers.

- Follow key customers and influence makers. (Chances are they'll follow you back—another plus.)

Set Up Collaborative Pinboards

When you identify particularly influential customers and opinion makers, invite them to collaborate on one of their boards. This way you bring additional content to your boards, as well as outside viewpoints. (Plus, you'll gain some of these person's followers as your own.)

Encourage Customer Pins

You definitely want to encourage your customers and other Pinterest users to pin items from your website, and to repin items you've pinned to your Pinterest boards. One particularly interesting approach is to encourage (and potentially reward) customers to pin pictures of themselves with one of your products, and then tag your company in those pins. You can then repin the photos on a special "customers only" pinboard.

Keep Adding New Boards

Yes, you created a set number of pinboards when you established your company's Pinterest account. You don't have to be limited to these boards, however. Over time, find reasons to create new pinboards, and thus add to your Pinterest presence.

For example, you might want to create a new pinboard when you launch a new line or brand. You might also want to create seasonal pinboards, either for products geared for a particular season (swimsuits, for example) or for season-specific uses of a given product. Think of a New Year's Eve board, for example, if you sell drink ingredients or party supplies, or a Summer Gardening board if you sell landscaping supplies or services. For that matter, an all-purpose Christmas Gifts board is great for just about any type of product. Use your imagination; there's always a good reason to create a new pinboard.

A Valentine's Day pinboard from Nordstrom (www.pinterest.com/nordstrom/)

Coupons Board

If you offer online or in-store coupons, create a board with pins to those coupons. Just remember to delete pins to coupons as they expire!

Become a Source of Industry News and Info

Your site doesn't have to be all about products and prices. You can also establish your company's reputation by becoming a key resource for industry news and information. That means creating a board for "industry news," and populating with pins (and repins) from various sources about interesting items and trends. Make your pinboard the go-to place for people who are interested in what's going on in your industry.

Use Keywords and Hashtags

Remember to make your pins more discoverable by incorporating keywords in the descriptive copy. (That's how people find most pins—by searching.) For those keywords that you think customers might want to search further, turn them into clickable hashtags by adding the # character before the word. Hashtags make your pins more useful, which customers will remember.

Remember the Images

As important as the pin description is, the image you pin is more important. Pinterest is a visual site, and people browse it with their eyes. That means pinning attractive images and making sure those images are eye-popping at thumbnail size. You want to entice users to click your pin thumbs, which means paying particular attention to the photos you choose.

Pin Videos as Well as Pictures

Many folks tend to forget that you can pin both images and videos to Pinterest. Get a leg up on your competition by pinning any YouTube videos you've created for your products, as well as any useful related videos from other YouTube users. Video adds variety to your pinboards—and provides unique value to your customers.

A how-to video pinned by PoppySeed Fabric (www.pinterest.com/poppyseedf/)

Let Your Staff Pin

Who should pin for your company? It could be anyone, but the task typically falls to someone in the marketing department. That doesn't mean you have to limit your pinning to one person, however; you can lighten the chore and broaden the content by allowing and encouraging multiple people from within your company to contribute. Just make your boards collaborative and invite the people you want to pin; give them a pinning schedule and have at it.

Add Prices to Your Pins

If you're pinning products that you're selling (or that your retailers are selling), go ahead and include the product price in the description. When you add a dollar or Euro sign in front of the price, Pinterest automatically adds a banner displaying that price. It certainly positions the pin as something of interest for people in the market for that item.

A priced pin from Gravel Ghost Vintage (www.pinterest.com/gravelghostvtg/)

Pinterest's Gifts Category

Another benefit to adding prices to your pins is that any pin with a price is likely to be displayed in Pinterest's Gifts category—which is welcome added exposure.

Measuring Your Success

When you incorporate Pinterest as part of your company's overall marketing strategy, you need to track the effectiveness of your efforts. Fortunately, there are many ways to do so.

First, and most obvious, is to track the number of followers you have on the Pinterest site. The more followers you have, the more opportunity you have to convert those followers into paying customers.

Tracking the number of followers

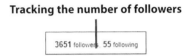

It's also good to track your overall exposure on Pinterest—beyond your own boards. Do this by going to the following URL:

www.pinterest.com/source/*yourcompanysite.com*

Just replace *yourcompanysite.com* with your own site's URL, and Pinterest displays all the pins made from your company's website.

Pinned images from Kate Spade's website (www.katespade.com)

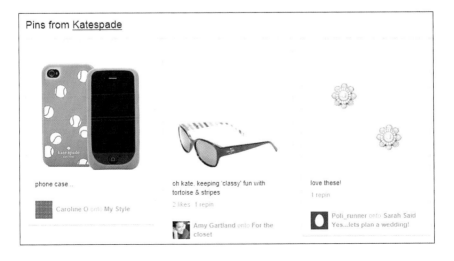

You can also track engagement, although it's a more nebulous metric. Count the number of likes, comments, and repins you receive, as well as the contents of those comments. The more positive engagement you get, the better.

Finally, if you're selling items online, you want to track the traffic from Pinterest to your website and the ultimate conversions you receive—that is, the percent of said traffic that ends up making a purchase online. You can track traffic using Google Analytics and other website analytics programs; conversions are tracked internally, by analyzing your online sales.

If you put in the effort, you're likely to find that Pinterest is a valuable component of your online marketing plan. It's all about connecting visually and socially—which Pinterest does with flair!

Editing your Pinterest profile information

Edit Profile

Email		Not shown publicly
Notifications	**Change Email Settings**	
Password	**Change Password**	
First name	Michael	
Last name	Miller	
Username	molehillgroup	http://pinterest.com/username
About	Michael Miller is a popular writer, with more than 100 how-to books published in the past two decades. Look for his upcoming book, MY PINTEREST, at a	

In this chapter, you learn how to edit your Pinterest account settings—and delete your Pinterest account.

→ Editing your profile information

→ Changing your profile picture

→ Changing your account password

→ Disabling email notifications

→ Hiding your account from search engines

→ Deleting your Pinterest account

Managing Your Pinterest Account

Now that you know how to use Pinterest, it's time to focus on a little account maintenance. Pinterest doesn't keep a lot of personal information about you (it's personal profiles are much less informative—or intrusive—than you find with Facebook and other social networking sites), but you probably want to review and fine-tune what's there. That includes choosing your profile picture, editing what personal information is displayed, and determining what sort of things Pinterest notifies you via email about. You can even choose to hide your Pinterest account from Google and other search engines or, if you're done with the whole thing, delete your Pinterest account.

Editing Your Profile Information

If you signed up for Pinterest using your Facebook or Twitter account, Pinterest grabs information from that account to create your initial Pinterest profile. You can, of course, edit this profile information at any time, or just add information that wasn't there to begin with.

>>>*step-by-step*

1. Click your name at the far right side of the Pinterest navigation bar.

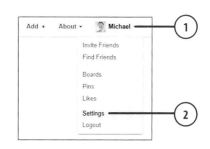

2. Click Settings from the drop-down menu to display the Edit Profile page.

3. To change your email address, enter a new address into the Email box.

4. To change your name, enter a new first or last name into the First Name and Last Name boxes.

5. To change your Pinterest username, enter a new name into the Username box.

Name Change

If you change your Pinterest username, anyone following you under your old name is still linked to you with your new username.

6. Enter a short description of yourself into the About box.

7. Enter your location (city and state) into the Location box.

8. If you have your own website or blog, enter that URL into the Website box.

Optional Information

Beyond your name, username, and email address, all the other information you enter into your Pinterest profile is optional.

9. When you're done entering or editing information, scroll to the bottom of the page and click the red Save Profile button.

Adding or Changing Your Profile Picture

Most Pinterest users like to display a picture of themselves or their work as a profile picture. If you signed up via Facebook or Twitter, Pinterest automatically used your picture from that account as your profile picture. You can, however, add or change profile pictures at any time.

>>>step-by-step

1. Click your name at the far right side of the Pinterest navigation bar.

2. Click Settings from the drop-down menu to display the Edit Profile page.

3. Scroll to the Image section and click the Upload an Image button.

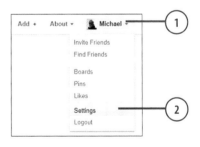

Refresh from Facebook

If you signed up for Pinterest via Facebook and have since changed your Facebook profile picture, you can add that new picture to your Pinterest profile by clicking the Refresh from Facebook button. You can also use your Twitter picture by clicking the Refresh from Twitter button.

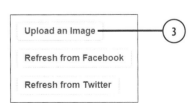

4. Click the Browse or Choose File button to display the Choose File to Upload or Open dialog box.

5. Navigate to and select the picture you want to use and then click the Open button.

6. Scroll to the bottom of the Edit Profile page and click the red Save Profile button.

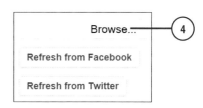

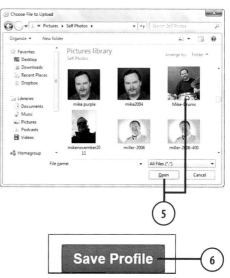

Changing Your Account Password

It's good security to change your online passwords on a regular basis. This helps prevent hackers from guessing your password and hacking into your account.

CREATING A STRONG PASSWORD

The longer the password you create, the more secure it is. (It's harder to guess a longer password than a shorter one.) In addition, you can create a more secure password by using a combination of letters, numbers, and special characters. Avoid easily guessed words or phrases; it's better to use nonsense words or codes. In general, the harder you make it for someone to guess a password, the more secure your account will be.

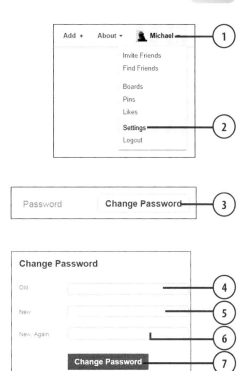

1. Click your name at the far right side of the Pinterest navigation bar.

2. Click Settings from the drop-down menu to display the Edit Profile page.

3. Scroll to the Password section and click the Change Password button to display the Change Password page.

4. Enter your current password into the Old box.

5. Enter your new password into the New box.

6. Enter your new password a second time into the New, Again box.

7. Click the red Change Password button.

Turning Off Pinterest's Email Notifications

Pinterest likes to notify you about new things. By default, Pinterest sends you email alerts when any of the following happens:

- Someone likes one of your pins
- Someone comments on one of your pins
- Someone repins one of your pins
- A new pin is added to a group pinboard
- Another users starts following you

In addition, Pinterest sends you news updates and a summary of your weekly activity—all via email.

If you'd rather not receive all of the notifications, you can configure Pinterest to only notify you under specified conditions—or not at all.

>>>*step-by-step*

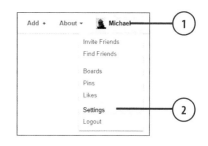

1. Click your name at the far right side of the Pinterest navigation bar.

2. Click Settings from the drop-down menu to display the Edit Profile page.

3. Go to the Notifications section and click the Change Email Settings button to display the Email Settings page.

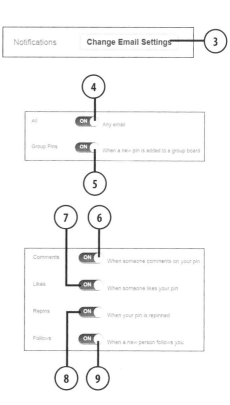

4. To turn off all notifications, click "off" the All switch.

5. To turn off notifications about group pins, click "off" the Group Pins switch.

6. To turn off notifications when someone comments on a pin, click "off" the Comments switch.

7. To turn off notifications when someone likes a pin, click "off" the Likes switch.

8. To turn off notifications when someone repins one of your items, click "off" the Repins switch.

9. To turn off notifications when someone new follows you, click "off" the Follows switch.

10. To change the frequency of the emails Pinterest sends you, go to the Frequency section and select either Immediately (the default) or Once Daily.

11. To not receive a weekly digest of your Pinterest activity, click "off" the Digest switch.

12. To not receive Pinterest news and updates, click "off" the News switch.

13. When you've made all your changes, click the red Save Settings button.

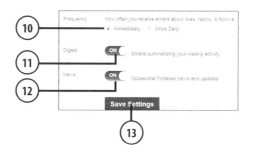

Hiding Your Pinterest Profile from Google and Other Search Engines

Google and other search engines are starting to include Pinterest in their web indexes. This means that someone searching for you might see your Pinterest profile and items you've pinned in their search results.

If you'd rather not have your Pinterest activity included in these web search results, you can choose to hide your Pinterest profile from Google and the other major search engines. This is often recommended if you want to keep the personal interests you display on Pinterest separate from your professional activities.

>>>step-by-step

1. Click your name at the far right side of the Pinterest navigation bar.

2. Click Settings from the drop-down menu to display the Edit Profile page.

3. Scroll to the Visibility section and click "off" the Visibility switch.

4. Click the red Save Profile button.

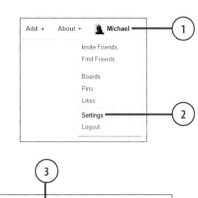

Deleting Your Pinterest Account

You might find, after a time, that Pinterest is no longer that interesting to you. If you haven't used Pinterest in a while, you can easily delete your entire Pinterest account.

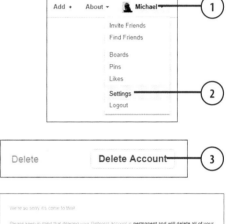

>>>*step-by-step*

1. Click your name at the far right side of the Pinterest navigation bar.

2. Click Settings from the drop-down menu to display the Edit Profile page.

3. Scroll to the Delete section at the bottom of the page and click the Delete Account button; this displays a new "delete my account" panel.

4. Check the Yes, I Want to Delete My Boards and Pins Permanently box.

5. Click the Delete My Account button.

It's Not All Good

DELETION IS PERMANENT

When you delete your account, you also delete all the boards and pins you've created—permanently. If you later decide to create a new account (you can't reactivate an old one), you have to re-add all those boards and pins again at that point in time.

Index

My
Pinterest

Safari
Books Online

FREE
Online Edition

que   Michael Miller

Your purchase of *My Pinterest* includes access to a free online edition for 45 days through the **Safari Books Online** subscription service. Nearly every Que book is available online through **Safari Books Online**, along with thousands of books and videos from publishers such as Addison-Wesley Professional, Cisco Press, Exam Cram, IBM Press, O'Reilly Media, Prentice Hall, Sams, and VMware Press.

Safari Books Online is a digital library providing searchable, on-demand access to thousands of technology, digital media, and professional development books and videos from leading publishers. With one monthly or yearly subscription price, you get unlimited access to learning tools and information on topics including mobile app and software development, tips and tricks on using your favorite gadgets, networking, project management, graphic design, and much more.

Activate your FREE Online Edition at
informit.com/safarifree

STEP 1:   Enter the coupon code: OMXAYYG.

STEP 2:   New Safari users, complete the brief registration form.
           Safari subscribers, just log in.

If you have difficulty registering on Safari or accessing the online edition,
please e-mail customer-service@safaribooksonline.com